Image Processing Recipes in MATLAB®

Leveraging the latest developments in MATLAB and its image processing toolbox, this 'cookbook' is a collection of 30 practical recipes for image processing, ranging from foundational techniques to recently published algorithms. Presented in a clear and meaningful sequence, these recipes are prepared with the reader in mind, allowing one to focus on particular topics or read as a whole from cover to cover.

Key Features:

- A practical, user-friendly guide that equips researchers and practitioners with the tools to implement efficient image processing workflows in MATLAB.
- Each recipe is presented through clear, step-by-step instructions and rich visual examples.
- Each recipe contains its own source code, explanations, and figures, making the book an excellent standalone resource for quick reference.
- Strategically structured to aid sequential learning, yet with self-contained chapters for those seeking solutions to specific image processing challenges.

The book serves as a concise and readable practical reference to deploy image processing pipelines in MATLAB quickly and efficiently. With its accessible and practical approach, the book is a valuable guide for those who navigate this evolving area, including researchers, students, developers, and practitioners in the fields of image processing, computer vision, and image analysis.

Oge Marques, PhD is a Professor of Computer Science and Engineering in the College of Engineering and Computer Science, a Professor of Biomedical Science (Secondary) in the Charles E. Schmidt College of Medicine, and a Professor of Information Technology (by courtesy), in the College of Business at Florida Atlantic University (FAU) (Boca Raton, FL).

He is the author of 12 technical books, one patent, and more than 130 refereed scientific articles on image processing, medical image analysis, computer vision, artificial intelligence, and machine learning.

Dr. Marques is a Senior Member of both the IEEE (Institute of Electrical and Electronics Engineers) and the ACM (Association for Computing Machinery), Fellow of the NIH AIM-AHEAD Consortium, Fellow of the Leshner Leadership Institute of the American Association for the Advancement of Science (AAAS), Tau Beta Pi Eminent Engineer, and member of the honor societies of Sigma Xi, Phi Kappa Phi, and Upsilon Pi Epsilon.

Gustavo Benvenutti Borba, PhD is an Associate Professor in the Department of Electronics and the Graduate School on Biomedical Engineering at the Federal University of Technology-Paraná (UTFPR) (Curitiba, Brazil).

He obtained his PhD in Electrical Engineering from UTFPR. He is the author of more than 30 refereed scientific articles on image processing, image retrieval, and related topics.

Chapman & Hall/CRC Computer Science and Engineering Recipes

Image Processing Recipes in MATLAB®
Oge Marques, Gustavo Benvenutti Borba

For more information on this series please visit: https://www.routledge.com /Chapman--HallCRC-Computer-Science-and-Engineering-Recipes-Series/ book-series

Image Processing Recipes in MATLAB®

Oge Marques
Gustavo Benvenutti Borba

CRC Press
Taylor & Francis Group
Boca Raton London New York

CRC Press is an imprint of the
Taylor & Francis Group, an **informa** business

A CHAPMAN & HALL BOOK

Designed cover image: © Shutterstock

MATLAB® and Simulink® are trademarks of The MathWorks, Inc. and are used with permission. The MathWorks does not warrant the accuracy of the text or exercises in this book. This book's use or discussion of MATLAB® or Simulink® software or related products does not constitute endorsement or sponsorship by The MathWorks of a particular pedagogical approach or particular use of the MATLAB® and Simulink® software.

First edition published 2024
by CRC Press
2385 NW Executive Center Drive, Suite 320, Boca Raton, FL 33431

and by CRC Press
4 Park Square, Milton Park, Abingdon, Oxon, OX14 4RN

CRC Press is an imprint of Taylor & Francis Group, LLC

© 2024 Oge Marques and Gustavo Benvenutti Borba

ISBN: 9780367771973 (hbk)
ISBN: 9780367767136 (pbk)
ISBN: 9781003170198 (ebk)

DOI: 10.1201/9781003170198

Typeset in Palatino
by Newgen Publishing UK

To Ingrid and Nicholas, with love
– OM

With love, to Maristela and Tito, who have filled me with motivation and encouragement
– GB

In loving memory of our dear friend and colleague Hugo Vieira Neto.

Contents

Part I   Basic image processing: Acquisition and visualization

Part II   Geometric operations

Part III   Histograms

Part IV   Point transformations

Part V   Spatial filtering and special effects

Part VI   Image segmentation

Part VII   Binary image analysis

Part VIII   Color image processing

Part IX   Batch processing and handling large images

Preface

This is a cookbook containing 30 recipes that showcase classic and modern image processing techniques using MATLAB. This book aims to provide a concise and easily understandable reference for deploying image processing pipelines quickly and efficiently in MATLAB. The recipes cover the latest developments in MATLAB and relevant toolboxes, including a wide range of image processing methods. These methods range from foundational techniques found in textbooks to popular contemporary algorithms.

This book is intended for researchers, students, developers, and practitioners in the area of visual media processing, such as computer vision, image processing, image and video analysis, image retrieval, and multimedia.

The recipes are organized into Parts and presented in a meaningful sequence to facilitate reading from cover to cover. Each recipe is self-contained and includes step-by-step instructions, source code, figures, brief discussions, and references for further learning.

This cookbook serves as both an introductory guide for novices in image processing and a succinct reference for seasoned practitioners. We're confident that its unique format makes it a worthy addition to your collection, either as an independent resource or alongside comprehensive texts in the field.

Recipes format

Figure 0.1 shows the general format of the recipes in the book. After the number and name of the recipe, you will find its *goal* and, eventually, meaningful information about that topic.

All the resources required to prepare the recipe are then listed in the **You will need (Ingredients)** section, including the version of the MATLAB and the Image Processing Toolbox (IPT), and image files. Most recipes use MATLAB's built-in images to streamline the preparation, while giving you the option to experiment with your images. When external images (available on GitHub: https://github.com/ip-recipes-matlab-book, including all code listings) are necessary, their filenames are indicated.

The core of the recipe is presented in the **Steps (Preparation)** section. It begins by objectively outlining the complete procedure to achieve the goal through a concise list of step-by-step instructions. Following the list, you will find detailed explanations of how to perform that image processing procedure, including annotated codes and figures. Depending on the recipe, this section is broken into subsections for better organization and flow.

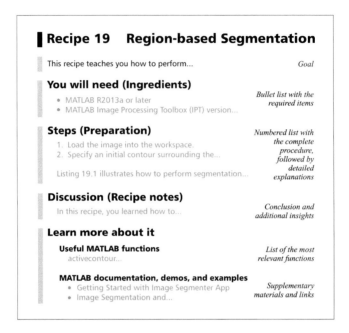

FIGURE 0.1
Format of the recipes throughout the book.

In the **Discussion (Recipe notes)** section, you will find a summary of the key points covered in the recipe, accompanied by insightful comments highlighting the most relevant theoretical and/or practical aspects of the image processing procedure.

The final section of each recipe is the **Learn more about it**, where you will discover a list containing the essential functions utilized in the recipe, along with other related functions worth exploring. Additionally, there is a curated list of related MATLAB official materials, including documentation, demos, and examples, all conveniently linked for further reference.

A note on MATLAB prerequisites and documentation

This book uses MATLAB and some of its toolboxes and apps to demonstrate practical approaches to image processing, encapsulated as 30 self-contained recipes.

If you need a MATLAB primer or refresher, we strongly recommend taking the following MATLAB short courses. These are free, interactive, browser-based, self-paced training programs that will guide you through the basics of MATLAB and some common Image Processing and Computer Vision procedures:

- MATLAB Onramp
  https://matlabacademy.mathworks.com/details/matlab-onramp/getti
  ngstarted
- Image Processing Onramp
  https://matlabacademy.mathworks.com/details/image-processing-
  onramp/imageprocessing

You might also want to bookmark the following resources, which should be useful for your explorations in MATLAB's image processing:

- Image Processing Toolbox "home"
  www.mathworks.com/help/images
- Comprehensive list of the Image Processing Toolbox functions
  www.mathworks.com/help/images/referencelist.html

Additionally, throughout the book, you will see references to valuable online resources from the MathWorks websites – including documentation, examples, and demos – that expand the discussion of the topics covered by each recipe and offer opportunities for further exploration on your own.

We wish you a pleasant reading and hope you will enjoy both the classic and spicier recipes that we have carefully prepared! Feel free to join our kitchen by sending us feedback and suggestions for additional titles in this series.

Acknowledgments

We are immensely grateful to many colleagues in the image processing community for their encouragement and valuable lessons throughout the years.

We are grateful to our current and former students who have provided valuable inspiration throughout many insightful conversations over the years, particularly Mikhail Anatholy Koslowski and Maiko Min Ian Lie.

A very special thank-you to our dear colleague and mentor Humberto Remigio Gamba, for his gentle leadership, unwavering support, continued encouragement, and friendship.

Special thanks to Christian Garbin, Matthew Acs and Richard Acs for their comments and suggestions during the preparation of this manuscript.

Many thanks to the MathWorks Book Program for their continued support over the years.

A very special note of gratitude to Randi (Cohen) Slack and her team at CRC Press / Taylor & Francis for their support throughout this project.

Part I

Basic image processing: Acquisition and visualization

Part I – Basic image processing: Acquisition and visualization

This Part contains recipes to get you started using MATLAB for image processing tasks and projects.

Recipe 1 shows how to read images from disk, display them, and save images to disk.

Recipe 2 teaches how to perform different types of image conversion.

Recipe 3 shows how to use a webcam to acquire your own images.

Recipe 4 introduces the *Image Browser* App and shows how it can be used to browse through image folders.

Following these recipes will give you the fundamental skills to acquire, read, write, browse, and visualize images using MATLAB.

1

Recipe 1: Loading, displaying, and saving images

This recipe teaches you how to load image contents from a file, display an image, and save the image contents back to disk.

You will need (Ingredients)

- MATLAB R2016b or later
- MATLAB Image Processing Toolbox (IPT) version R2016b or later
- (OPTIONAL[1]) One or more of your images

Steps (Preparation)

(OPTIONAL) Displaying information about an image file

MATLAB has a built-in function to display information about image files (without opening them and storing their contents in the workspace), imfinfo.

1. The code below shows how to read information about a built-in image file, pout.tif.

```
imfinfo('pout.tif')
```

The resulting structure (stored in variable ans) will contain the following information[2]:

```
        Filename: '/.../pout.tif'
     FileModDate: '13-Apr-2015 13:23:13'
        FileSize: 69296
          Format: 'tif'
           Width: 240
          Height: 291
        BitDepth: 8
```

```
                 ColorType: 'grayscale'
           FormatSignature: [73 73 42 0]
                 ByteOrder: 'little-endian'
            NewSubFileType: 0
            BitsPerSample: 8
               Compression: 'PackBits'
  PhotometricInterpretation: 'BlackIsZero'
               StripOffsets: [9x1 double]
            SamplesPerPixel: 1
               RowsPerStrip: 34
            StripByteCounts: [9x1 double]
                XResolution: 72
                YResolution: 72
             ResolutionUnit: 'Inch'
         PlanarConfiguration: 'Chunky'
                Orientation: 1
                  FillOrder: 1
            GrayResponseUnit: 0.0100
             MaxSampleValue: 255
             MinSampleValue: 0
               Thresholding: 1
                     Offset: 69004
           ImageDescription: Copyright The MathWorks, Inc.
```

Many of these fields are too technical, and some are file format-dependent. Nonetheless, you should still be able to locate information about the image size (240×291 pixels), the file size (69296 bytes), the type of image (grayscale), the number of bits per pixel (8), and its minimum and maximum values (0 and 255).

2. (OPTIONAL) Repeat the process for other built-in images.

3. Type the MATLAB code below and save it in a script.

LISTING 1.1
Displaying MATLAB demo images using the *Image Browser* App.

```
1  % Display MATLAB demo images using the Image Browser app
2  folder = fullfile(matlabroot, '/toolbox/images/imdata');
3  if exist(folder, 'dir')
4    fprintf('Demo Images Folder is %s.\n', folder);
5  else
6    fprintf('Folder %s does not exist.\n', folder);
7  end
8  dir(folder)
9  imageBrowser(folder)
```

The script in Listing 1.1 will display the demo images' file names in the command window and open the MATLAB *Image Browser* App[3], which allows you to browse the images and obtain additional information about them – file name, image size (rows × columns × number of color channels), and data class (Figure 1.1).

4. (OPTIONAL) Repeat the process for your image folders.

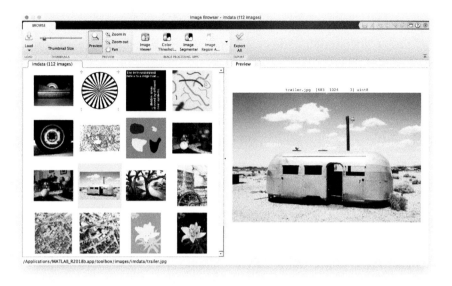

FIGURE 1.1
Using the *Image Browser* App to browse through demo images and obtain additional information about the `trailer.jpg` image.

Reading an image file (Loading an image from disk)

MATLAB has a built-in function to open and read the contents of image files in the most popular formats (e.g., TIFF, JPEG, BMP, GIF, and PNG), `imread`.

The `imread` function allows you to read image files of almost any type, in virtually any format, located anywhere[4]. This saves you from a (potentially large) number of problems associated with file headers, memory allocation, file format conventions, etc., and allows you to focus on what you want to do to the image once it has been read and stored into a variable in the MATLAB workspace.

When using `imread`, it is essential to know the image type (binary, grayscale, true color, indexed color, etc.) and assign the image's contents (after the file is read and decompressed) to the proper variable(s).

1. The code below shows how to read a built-in grayscale image – `pout.tif` – and assign its contents to a workspace variable, `img_1`.

```
img_1 = imread('pout.tif');
```

In this case, a single variable, `img_1`, on the left-hand side, is appropriate. Inspecting the size and numerical contents of `img_1`, you should see that it is a 2D array of size 291×240, whose values are unsigned integers within the [0, 255] range.

2. The code below shows how to read a built-in indexed color image – trees.tif – and assign its contents to two workspace variables: img_2 (containing the index) and map_img_2 (containing the associated colormap).

```
[img_2,map_img_2] = imread('trees.tif');
```

3. The code below shows how to read a built-in true color image – peppers.png – and assign its contents to a variable img_3 whose size is $M \times N \times 3$, indicating the pixel values for each pixel in each of the three (*R, G, and B*) channels, where M is the number of rows and N is the number of columns.

```
img_3 = imread('peppers.png');
```

4. (OPTIONAL) Repeat the process for other built-in images.

5. (OPTIONAL) Repeat the process for your images.

Displaying the contents of an image

MATLAB has several functions for displaying images:

- image: displays an image using the current colormap[5].
- imagesc: scales image data to the full range of the current colormap and displays the image.
- imshow: displays an image and contains several optimizations and optional parameters for property settings associated with the image display.
- imtool: calls the *Image Viewer* App tool from the command line. The *Image Viewer* App offers an integrated environment for displaying images, accessing several tools for navigating and exploring images and performing common image processing tasks.

Listing 1.2 shows how to open an image file and display it using different imshow options:

LISTING 1.2
Opening and displaying an image file.

```
1 % Open and display an image file
2 img_1 = imread('pout.tif');
3 imshow(img_1)
4 figure, imshow(img_1,[])
5 figure, imshow(img_1,[100 160])
```

The first call to imshow (line 3) displays the image in its original state. The code in line 4 opens a new figure and displays a scaled (for display purposes) version of the same image. The code in line 5 specifies a range of gray levels, such that all values between 100 and 160 will map to values between 0 and 255[6]. The three results are shown side-by-side in Figure 1.2.

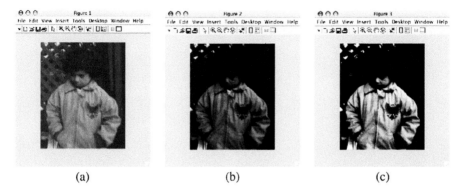

(a)   (b)   (c)

FIGURE 1.2

Displaying an image: (a) without scaling; (b) scaling for display purposes; (c) emphasizing pixels within a specified range. Original image: courtesy of The MathWorks.

Writing the resulting image onto a file

MATLAB has a built-in function, `imwrite`, to write the contents of an image to disk using any of the most popular graphic file formats (such as JPEG, PNG, or TIFF) as well as several legacy formats, e.g., PCX, PGM, and BMP.

If the output file format uses lossy compression (e.g., JPEG), `imwrite` allows the specification of a *quality* parameter, used as a trade-off between the resulting image's subjective quality and file size.

Listing 1.3 shows how to read an image from a PNG file and save it to a JPG file using three different quality parameters: 75 (default), 5 (poor quality, small size), and 95 (better quality, larger size).

LISTING 1.3

Image conversion at different quality settings.

```
% Image conversion (PNG->JPG) at different quality settings
img_4 = imread('peppers.png');
imwrite(img_4, 'pep75.jpg');
imwrite(img_4, 'pep05.jpg', 'quality', 5);
imwrite(img_4, 'pep95.jpg', 'quality', 95);
```

The results are displayed in Figure 1.3. The image in part (c) of the figure is clearly of lower visual quality than the ones in parts (b) and (d). On the other hand, the differences between the images in parts (b) and (d) are barely noticeable.

Discussion (Recipe notes)

In this recipe, you learned the basics of reading images from disk, displaying, and writing them (presumably in a different format, if you so desire) back to disk.

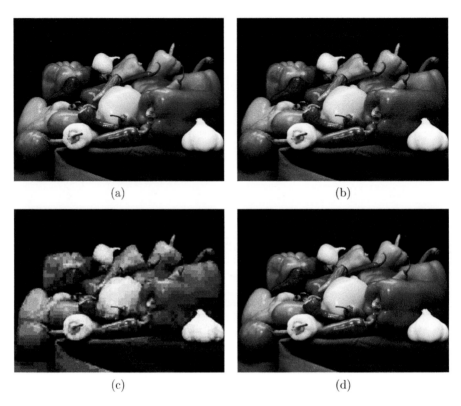

(a)   (b)

(c)   (d)

FIGURE 1.3
Reading and writing images: (a) original image (PNG); (b) compressed image (JPG, q = 75, file size = 24 KB); (c) compressed image (JPG, q = 5, file size = 8 KB); (d) compressed image (JPG, q = 95, file size = 60 KB). Original image: courtesy of The MathWorks.

One of the best features of MATLAB and its support for image processing is its ability to handle images of various formats; once the image is loaded into the workspace, it becomes a variable (matrix) that can be processed using many useful library functions.

Special attention must be given, however, to the fact that you must have a basic understanding of image types and their representation in MATLAB to assign images to the correct variables and process the pixel values in a way that is consistent with their range.

Learn more about it

Useful MATLAB functions

Type the function name in the search field at www.mathworks.com/help/matlab/

· image ^{7} · imagesc · imfinfo · imread · imshow · imwrite ·

MATLAB documentation, demos, and examples

- Add Color Bar to Displayed Grayscale Image
  www.mathworks.com/help/images/add-colorbar-to-displayed-image.
  html
- Display Different Image Types
  www.mathworks.com/help/images/display-different-image-types.html
- Displaying Image Data
  www.mathworks.com/help/matlab/creating_plots/displaying-image-
  data.html
- Image Browser App
  www.mathworks.com/help/images/ref/imagebrowser-app.html
- Image Types in the Toolbox
  www.mathworks.com/help/images/image-types-in-the-toolbox.html
- Image Viewer App
  www.mathworks.com/help/images/ref/imageviewer-app.html

Notes

1 The recipe has been prepared using MATLAB's built-in images.
2 All empty fields have been omitted for space reasons.
3 You will learn more about the *Image Browser* App in Recipe 4.
4 MATLAB also contains specialized functions for reading DICOM (Digital Imaging and Communications in Medicine) files (dicomread), NITF (National Imagery Transmission Format) files (nitfread), and HDR (high dynamic range) files (hdrread). They are beyond the scope of this recipe.
5 The colormap array is an M-by-3 matrix of class *double*, where each element is a floating-point value in the range [0, 1]. Each row in the colormap represents the R (red), G (green), and B (blue) values for that particular row.
6 This means that pixel values below 100 in the original image will become black pixels in the displayed image and pixel intensities above 160 in the original image will become white pixels in the displayed image.
7 There are several functions with the same name in MATLAB. In this case, we are interested in the one at: www.mathworks.com/help/matlab/ref/image.html.

2

Recipe 2: Image conversion

This recipe teaches you how to perform three types of image conversions: (1) convert an image file to a different *file format*; (2) convert an image to a different *type*; and (3) convert an image to a different *class*.

You will need (Ingredients)

- MATLAB R2020b or later
- MATLAB Image Processing Toolbox (IPT) version R2020b or later
- (OPTIONAL[1]) One or more of your images

Steps (Preparation)

Part 1: File format conversion

MATLAB has no library function to perform (batch) file format conversion. Consequently, you have to follow these steps:

1. Specify the original and desired file formats.
2. Loop through the contents of the folder where the images reside.
3. For each image, read the file in the original format from disk and save it in the desired file format.

An image can be read from disk using `imread` and saved back to disk using `imwrite`[2].

Part 2: Conversion to a different image type

Conversion between different image types, such as RGB (truecolor), binary, grayscale, and indexed images, can be achieved using built-in library functions, such as those listed in Table 2.1.

DOI: 10.1201/9781003170198-3

TABLE 2.1

MATLAB functions to perform image data class conversion.

Name	Description
cmap2gray	Convert RGB colormap to grayscale colormap
gray2ind	Convert grayscale or binary image to indexed image
im2gray	Convert RGB image to grayscale
ind2gray	Convert indexed image to grayscale image
mat2gray	Convert matrix to grayscale image
rgb2gray	Convert RGB image or colormap to grayscale
rgb2lightness	Convert RGB color values to lightness values
rgb2ind	Convert RGB image to indexed image
ind2rgb	Convert indexed image to RGB image
label2rgb	Convert label matrix into RGB image
demosaic	Convert Bayer pattern encoded image to truecolor image
imsplit	Split multichannel image into its individual channels

Part 3: Conversion to a different image class

Once the contents of an image have been read and stored into one or more variables, you are encouraged to inspect the data class of these variables and their range of values to understand *how* the pixel contents are represented and what is their allowed range of values. You should ensure that the variable's data class is compatible with the input data class expected by the MATLAB functions that will be applied to that variable. If you are writing your own functions and scripts, you must also ensure data class compatibility or perform the necessary conversions.

The most common data classes for images in MATLAB are:

- uint8: 1 byte (8 bits) per pixel per channel, where each pixel value is represented within the [0, 255] range.

- uint16: 2 bytes (16 bits) per pixel per channel, where each pixel value is represented within the [0, 65535] range.

- int16: 2 bytes (16 bits) per pixel per channel, where each pixel value is represented within the [-32768, 32767] range.

- single: 4 bytes (32 bits) per pixel per channel, i.e., single-precision floating-point values, usually in the [0.0, 1.0] range.

- double (the default numeric data type (class) in MATLAB): 8 bytes (64 bits) per pixel per channel, i.e., double-precision floating-point values, usually in the [0.0, 1.0] range.

- logical: 1 byte per pixel, representing its value as *true* (1 or white) or *false* (0 or black).

To convert an image (or an arbitrary array, for that matter) to a data class and range suitable for image processing, you are encouraged to use one of the specialized functions listed in Table 2.2.

TABLE 2.2

IPT functions to perform image data class conversion.

Name	Description
im2double	Convert image to double precision
im2int16	Convert image to 16-bit signed integers
im2single	Convert image to single precision
im2uint16	Convert image to 16-bit unsigned integers
im2uint8	Convert image to 8-bit unsigned integers

Note that functions such as im2double and im2single **do not** rescale the output to the [0.0, 1.0] range when the input image has single or double data type. If your input image is of data type single or double with pixel values outside this range, you can use the rescale function to scale pixel values to the expected range.

Discussion (Recipe notes)

In this recipe, you learned three types of conversions that might be needed when dealing with images in MATLAB:

1. File format conversions, essentially accomplished using (a series of) imread and imwrite function calls.

2. Image type conversions, for which there are several convenient built-in functions (Table 2.1).

3. Image class (data type) conversions, for which there are several built-in functions (Table 2.2).

As mentioned in Recipe 1, one of the best features of MATLAB is its ability to handle images of various formats and classes. In this recipe, we have expanded upon the need to have a basic understanding of data types (classes) in MATLAB in order to ensure that pixel values are represented using the appropriate numerical precision and within an expected range of values. This is particularly crucial in the case of images of type single or double – where the values are typically within the [0.0, 1.0] range, whereas the corresponding data classes are capable of representing much larger and smaller (i.e., negative) values.

Learn more about it

Useful MATLAB functions

Type the function name in the search field at www.mathworks.com/help/matlab/

· cmap2gray · demosaic · gray2ind · im2double · im2gray
· im2single · imread · imsplit · imwrite · ind2gray · ind2rgb
· label2rgb · mat2gray · rescale · rgb2gray · rgb2ind ·
rgb2lightness ·

MATLAB documentation, demos, and examples

- Convert Between Image Types
  www.mathworks.com/help/images/convert-between-image-types.html
- Convert Image Data Between Data Types
  www.mathworks.com/help/images/convert-image-data-between-classes.
  html
- Display Separated Color Channels of RGB Image
  www.mathworks.com/help/images/display-separated-color-channels-
  of-rgb-image.html
- Image Types in the Toolbox
  www.mathworks.com/help/images/image-types-in-the-toolbox.html

Notes

1 The recipe has been prepared using MATLAB's built-in images.
2 See Recipe 1 for additional details.

3

Recipe 3: Image acquisition using a webcam

This recipe teaches you different ways to acquire images from a computer's built-in webcam or from a webcam attached to the USB (Universal Serial Bus) port.

USB Video Class (UVC) devices, such as integrated or external USB webcams, can serve as valuable tools for image processing tasks. These webcams, commonly found in most computer setups, offer sufficient quality for a wide array of applications and are conveniently accessible via MATLAB. Even when your project demands the use of more advanced cameras, possibly even requiring specific optical or lighting configurations, leveraging readily available resources to conduct quick and simple experiments can be beneficial. This approach not only enables you to preview the potential image processing strategies for a particular application but also to gain insights into the ideal lighting setup or the desirable characteristics of an alternative image capturing device.

You will need (Ingredients)

- MATLAB R2019b or later
- MATLAB Image Processing Toolbox (IPT) version R2019b or later
- A built-in webcam or a webcam attached to a USB port
- (OPTIONAL) MATLAB Image Acquisition Toolbox (IAT) version R2019b or later

Steps (Preparation)

1. Install the Hardware Support Package *USB webcams*.
2. Get a list of the available webcams in the system.

DOI: 10.1201/9781003170198-4

3. Preview, acquire, store in the workspace, and display images from the desired webcam.

4. Connect, get, and set parameters of the desired webcam.

The *Hardware Support Package for USB webcams* allows MATLAB to communicate with the webcams in your system. Starting from MATLAB 2014a, several Support Packages are not included in MATLAB installation but are available for download and installation through the *Add-Ons* menu of the desktop instead. To download and install the Hardware Support Package for USB webcams, proceed as follows:

1. Click on *HOME* tab → *Add-Ons* → *Get Hardware Support Packages*.

2. In the *Hardware Support Packages* window, search for webcam. The top result should be *MATLAB Support Package for USB Webcams*.

3. (*If the support package isn't installed yet*) Click on the *Install* button and follow the instructions until the installation is finished.

Examples

Now you should be able to interface with the available webcams and acquire images, using the code in Listing 3.1[1].

LISTING 3.1
Webcam – basic setup.

```
% Webcam - basic setup
myWcams = webcamlist
wcam1 = webcam(1)
% wcam2 = webcam(2)
img_1 = snapshot(wcam1);
% img_2 = snapshot(wcam2);
image(img_1)
% figure, image(img_2)
clear wcam1
% clear wcam2
```

The webcamlist function lists the system's webcams that MATLAB can access:

```
myWcams =
    'Integrated Webcam'
    'Logitech HD Webcam C270'
```

The webcam function creates *webcam objects*, into variables wcam1 and wcam2. In the workspace, note that their class is webcam. These are the most important variables in our code since they represent the connection between

MATLAB and webcams. The `wcam1` and `wcam2` variables contain properties and their respective values for each webcam. The listed properties and values are device-specific, for example:

```
wcam1 =
  webcam with properties:

                       Name: 'Integrated Webcam'
                 Resolution: '640x480'
       AvailableResolutions: {'640x480'  '160x120'  '320x180'
                              '320x240'  '424x240'  '640x360'}
                        Hue: 0
                   Exposure: -5
                   Contrast: 0
                 Saturation: 64
           WhiteBalanceMode: 'auto'
                 Brightness: 0
                  Sharpness: 2
                      Gamma: 100
               WhiteBalance: 4600
       BacklightCompensation: 1
               ExposureMode: 'auto'

wcam2 =
  webcam with properties:

                       Name: 'Logitech HD Webcam C270'
                 Resolution: '640x480'
       AvailableResolutions: {1x19 cell}
                   Exposure: -4
                   Contrast: 32
                 Saturation: 32
                 Brightness: 128
                       Gain: 192
                  Sharpness: 24
               WhiteBalance: 5690
       BacklightCompensation: 0
               ExposureMode: 'auto'
```

This confirms that the communication between MATLAB and the webcams is operational. MATLAB has been granted access to the live video from the webcam, i.e., a sequence of frames captured by the webcam at a specific, device-dependent timing between the frames, expressed in *frames per second* (FPS). The acquisition of a single image means we are selecting one of those frames as our *still image*. This is obtained with `snapshot`, which triggers storing a single frame in the workspace. The `snapshot` function receives a *webcam object* as an input parameter and outputs an image. It is a good practice to `clear` the *webcam object* variables once the connection is no longer needed to make the associated webcam available for further connections.

In Listing 3.2 (which uses `Integrated Webcam`), we improve the usability of Listing 3.1. The `preview` function opens the MATLAB *Video Preview* window, which shows the live video provided by the webcam. The `pause` function stops the script execution and waits for the user to press any key. After a key is pressed, the `snapshot` function is executed, triggering a single image acquisition and making it available in the workspace.

LISTING 3.2

Webcam – improved setup.

```
1  % Webcam - improved setup
2  wcam = webcam(1);
3  preview(wcam)
4  disp('Press any key to trigger acquisiton')
5  pause
6  img_1 = snapshot(wcam);
7  imshow(img_1)
8  clear wcam
```

Listing 3.3 shows how to acquire an image sequence by placing the `snapshot` function in a loop. In this case, four RGB true color (24 bits per pixel) images are stored in a four-dimensional (4D) array, where the fourth dimension is used to address each image[2]. See Figure 3.1 for examples of results.

The code in Listing 3.3 can be useful in applications that require the analysis of a sequence of images from a given dynamic event. This strategy can also be used to allow further selection of the best image among the n available candidates or in situations in which it is difficult to trigger the acquisition of the single desired image manually.

LISTING 3.3

Webcam – image sequence acquisition.

```
1  % Webcam - image sequence acquisition
2  wcam = webcam(1);
3  preview(wcam)
4  disp('Press any key to trigger acquisiton')
5  pause
6  img_array = [];
7  for n = 1:4
8      img_array = cat(4,img_array,snapshot(wcam));
9  end
10 montage(img_array), title('Four acquired images')
11 img_3 = img_array(:,:,:,3);
12 figure, imshow(img_3), title('The third acquired image')
13 clear wcam
```

Four acquired images

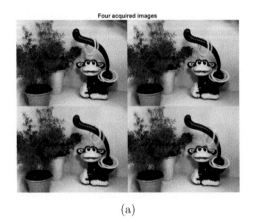

The third acquired image

(a)   (b)

FIGURE 3.1

Examples of using the snapshot function in a loop to acquire a sequence of images. Part (a) shows the four images obtained inside the loop; it is possible to observe, from the sequence of images (left to right, top to bottom), that the disks are sliding down the monkey's tail. Part (b) shows a specific image (lines 11–12 in Listing 3.3).

Discussion (Recipe notes)

In this recipe, you learned how to acquire images using a webcam and the basic functionality provided by MATLAB to identify, connect, and control the webcams available in your system.

The Image Acquisition Toolbox (IAT) extends MATLAB's image acquisition functionalities, including interfacing with several industry-standard devices, such as optical, depth, infrared, and 3D cameras; frame grabbers; X-ray detectors; and 3D laser line profile scanners.

Learn more about it

Useful MATLAB functions

Type the function name in the search field at www.mathworks.com/help/matlab/

· closePreview · preview · snapshot · webcam · webcamlist ·

MATLAB documentation, demos, and examples

- Acquiring a Single Image in a Loop Using getsnapshot
  https://www.mathworks.com/help/imaq/acquire-single-image-in-loop-using-getsnapshot.html

- Configuring Callback Properties
  www.mathworks.com/help/imaq/configuring-callback-properties.html
- Determining the Rate of Acquisition
  www.mathworks.com/help/imaq/determining-the-rate-of-acquisition.html
- Event Types (Supported by the Image Acquisition Toolbox)
  www.mathworks.com/help/imaq/event-types.html
- Image Acquisition Toolbox Properties
  www.mathworks.com/help/imaq/image-acquisition-toolbox-properties.html
- Logging Data at Constant Intervals
  www.mathworks.com/help/imaq/logging-data-at-constant-intervals.html
- MATLAB Support Package for USB Webcams
  www.mathworks.com/help/supportpkg/usbwebcams/index.html
- Retrieving Event Information
  www.mathworks.com/help/imaq/retrieving-event-information.html
- Set Properties for Webcam Acquisition
  www.mathworks.com/help/supportpkg/usbwebcams/ug/set-properties-for-webcam-acquisition.html

---

Notes

1   If your computer has two webcams, such as the one used in this example, uncomment lines 4, 6, 8, and 10.
2   Other approaches could be used, such as storing each image in a cell of a cell array or in a field of an array of structures. However, in this example, the option for the 4D array was chosen in anticipation of using the montage function, which expects this type of data structure.

4

Recipe 4: Browsing through images

This recipe teaches you how to browse through images in a folder and sub-folders, preview images, and automatically get information about the image files to access them.

In Recipe 1, we briefly introduced the *Image Browser* App. We indicated how it can be helpful to visualize images and obtain additional information about them, such as file name, image size, and data class. This recipe will expand our discussion and introduce the `ImageDatastore` object.

We will use the *Image Browser* App to explore Caltech 101, a well-known image dataset created in September 2003 to advance research in object recognition that consists of a total of 9144 color images with a resolution of 300×200 pixels, organized into 101 object categories, such as animals, vehicles, and people.

You will need (Ingredients)

- MATLAB R2016b or later
- MATLAB Image Processing Toolbox (IPT) version R2016b or later
- Caltech 101 image dataset

Steps (Preparation)

1. Download and extract the Caltech 101 image dataset.
2. Open the *Image Browser* App, and use it to browse and preview the downloaded image dataset.
3. Export an image and an `ImageDatastore` object from the *Image Browser* to the workspace.
4. Create an `ImageDatastore` object using the `imageDatastore` function.

      DOI: 10.1201/9781003170198-5

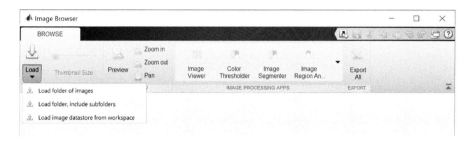

FIGURE 4.1

Image Browser: loading images. Three options are available under *Load*. The option *Load folder, include subfolders* was selected.

To get started, go to the *Download* section of the Caltech 101 image dataset website[1], download the `caltech-101.zip` file and extract it, locate the `101_ObjectCategories.tar.gz` file, and extract it at a path of your preference. The required disk space is ≈150 MB. In MATLAB, open the *Image Browser* App, either by selecting it from the *APPS* tab at the MATLAB desktop or by typing `imageBrowser` in the Command Window.

Figure 4.1 shows the GUI and the available options when you click the *Load* button:

- *Load folder of images*: *Image Browser* loads the images of a single folder. It does not include subfolders.

- *Load folder, include subfolders*: *Image Browser* loads the images of the selected folder and its subfolders.

- *Load image datastore from workspace*: *Image Browser* loads a `ImageDatastore` object which contains, among other information, images' file names and locations.

Select the *Load folder, include subfolders* option, and browse your computer using the *Select a folder with images* window to indicate the Caltech 101 "root folder", `101_ObjectCategories`, as depicted in Figure 4.2[2]. Finish by clicking on the *Select Folder* button. All 9144 images can now be browsed using the *Image Browser*.

You can visualize the images' thumbnails (Figure 4.3(a)) and adjust their sizes using the *Thumbnail Size* slider (Figure 4.3(b)).

You can inspect the image by double-clicking on it or clicking on *Preview* (see Figure 4.4).

With a right-click on the image in the browsing or preview areas, it is possible to select the *Export image to workspace* option, and a dialog box allows you to type the variable name. The selected image becomes available in the workspace after clicking *OK* at the dialog box.

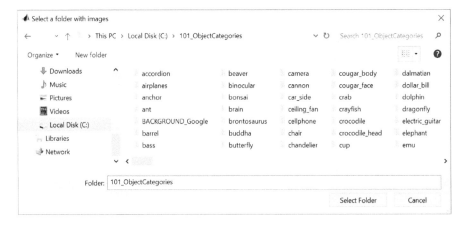

FIGURE 4.2
Image Browser: after selecting the *Load folder, include subfolders* option, a window to browse the computer and select the desired folder is provided.

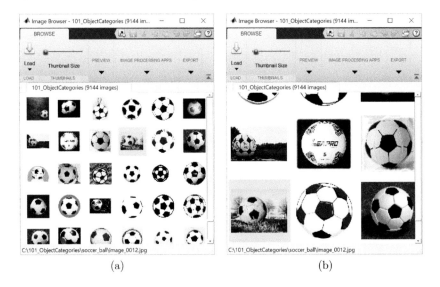

(a)   (b)

FIGURE 4.3
Image Browser: thumbnails. After selecting a folder, it is possible to browse through images (a) and adjust thumbnails' sizes at the *Thumbnail Size* slider (b).

The *Image Browser* App also provides the *Export All* option that generates a MATLAB object of the `ImageDatastore` class. Clicking on *Export All*, a dialog box allows you to type the name of the variable of the class `ImageDatastore` to be exported to the workspace. In this case, the name `x101_ObjectCategories` is suggested. Click on the *OK* button to finish.

FIGURE 4.4
Image Browser: preview. The selected image and its name, size, and class are presented in the
Preview area.

Typing `x101_ObjectCategories` in the Command Window to get the
contents of the variable, we have:

```
x101_ObjectCategories =
  ImageDatastore with properties:

        Files: {
            'C:\101_ObjectCategories\BACKGROUND_Google\image_0001.jpg';
            'C:\101_ObjectCategories\BACKGROUND_Google\image_0002.jpg';
            'C:\101_ObjectCategories\BACKGROUND_Google\image_0003.jpg'
            ... and 9141 more
              }
     ReadSize: 1
       Labels: {}
      ReadFcn: @iptui.internal.imageBrowser.readAllIPTFormats
```

The field `Files` is an array of cells that provides the location and file name
(complete path) of each of the 9144 images of the dataset since we loaded
the entire dataset into the *Image Browser*. To generate an `ImageDatastore`
object of a single object category, for instance, *water lily flower*, follow the steps
in Figure 4.1, but now load into *Image Browser* the subfolder `water_lilly`,
and proceed with a new *Export All*. Accepting the suggested variable name of
the dialog box, a new `ImageDatastore` is exported to the workspace, with
the name `water_lilly`. Typing `water_lilly` in the Command Window
to get the content of the variable, you should see the complete paths of the
37 images:

```
water_lilly =
  ImageDatastore with properties:

        Files: {
                'C:\101_ObjectCategories\water_lilly\image_0001.jpg';
                'C:\101_ObjectCategories\water_lilly\image_0002.jpg';
                'C:\101_ObjectCategories\water_lilly\image_0003.jpg'
                ... and 34 more
               }
     ReadSize: 1
       Labels: {}
      ReadFcn: @iptui.internal.imageBrowser.readAllIPTFormats
```

An image can now be read, loaded into the workspace, and displayed with the following commands:

```
filename = water_lilly.Files{30};
img_1 = imread(filename);
figure, imshow(img_1)
```

The same operation can be performed using the `readimage` function, which accepts an `ImageDatastore` object and a number indicating the index of the complete path in the `Files` field:

```
[img_2,fileinfo] = readimage(water_lilly,30);
figure, imshow(img_2)
```

Listing 4.1 shows how to create `ImageDatastore` objects programmatically using the `imageDatastore` function. In this case, we get information about the entire dataset and select only those from the `water_lilly` subfolder using the `Labels` field, whose values were filled automatically, passing the *name-value pair arguments* `'LabelSource'`, `'foldernames'` to the `imageDatastore` function. This strategy helps to improve the organization of the image datastore and makes it easier to access images of a given label.

LISTING 4.1
ImageDatastore creation and processing.

```
1  % ImageDatastore creation and processing
2  imds_path = '101_ObjectCategories';
3  imds = imageDatastore(imds_path,'IncludeSubfolders',true,... 'LabelSource','foldernames');
4  idx = find(imds.Labels == 'water_lilly');
5  WLpaths = imds.Files(idx);
6  filename = WLpaths{30};
7  img_3 = imread(filename);
8  figure, imshow(img_3)
```

The automatically created labels can now be inspected as follows:

```
autoLabels = imds.Labels;
```

The `autoLabels` array is of class `categorical`[3]. To get a list of the labels, we can use the `unique` function:

```
uLabels = unique(imds.Labels)
```

The `ImageDatastore` object is a valuable and versatile resource, particularly when dealing with many image files. In this recipe, we used the `readimage` function provided by the `ImageDatastore` object, but there are other functions that you might want to explore. For example, `countEachLabel` provides the number of files per label in a variable of the class `table`:

```
tableLabels = countEachLabel(imds)
```

```
tableLabels =
  102x2 table
            Label         Count

    BACKGROUND_Google       467
    Faces                   435
    Faces_easy              435
    Leopards                200
    Motorbikes              798
    accordion                55
    airplanes               800
    anchor                   42
    . . .                   . . .
    windsor_chair            56
    wrench                   39
    yin_yang                 60
```

Discussion (Recipe notes)

In this recipe, you learned how to use the *Image Browser* App to browse and preview images from a folder and its subfolders. You also learned how to create an object of the `ImageDatastore` class in two different ways: (i) using the *Export All* option of the *Image Browser*; and (ii) using the `imageDatastore` function.

We encourage you to explore further the *Image Browser* App and the `ImageDatastore` class using some of the resources listed next.

Learn more about it

Useful MATLAB functions

Type the function name in the search field at www.mathworks.com/help/matlab/
· `countEachLabel` · `imageDatastore` · `readimage` ·

MATLAB documentation, demos, and examples

- Class (data type) `categorical`
  www.mathworks.com/help/matlab/ref/categorical.html
- Class (data type) `table`
  www.mathworks.com/help/matlab/ref/table.html
- Image Browser
  www.mathworks.com/help/images/ref/imagebrowser-app.html
- Image file formats supported by MATLAB
  www.mathworks.com/help/matlab/ref/imformats.html
- View and Edit Collection of Images in Folder or Datastore
  www.mathworks.com/help/images/view-thumbnails-of-images-in-folder-or-datastore.html

Notes

1 https://data.caltech.edu/records/mzrjq-6wc02
2 Note that each subfolder of the image dataset is named with the category of the object. Thus, we should expect 101 subfolders within `101_ObjectCategories`, but there are 102, as we will see later. The `BACKGROUND_Google` subfolder was created by the authors for evaluation of the proposed object recognition algorithm [17], and it is not considered an object category.
3 For more information about the `categorical` data type, check the *Learn more about it* section at the end of this recipe.

Part II

Geometric operations

DOI: 10.1201/9781003170198-6

Part II – Geometric operations

This Part contains recipes that focus on image processing techniques that modify the geometric properties of an image, i.e., the spatial relationships between groups of pixels.

Recipe 5 shows how to perform basic geometric operations on images, such as cropping, flipping, resizing, and rotating.

Recipe 6 teaches how to create affine transformations specifying arbitrary geometric operations and apply them to images.

5

Recipe 5: Geometric transformations

This recipe teaches you how to perform basic geometric operations on images.

Geometric operations modify the geometry of an image by repositioning pixels in a constrained way. In other words, rather than changing the *pixel values* of an image (as most techniques presented in the rest of this book do), they modify the *spatial relationships* between groups of pixels.

You will need (Ingredients)

- MATLAB R2014a or later
- MATLAB Image Processing Toolbox (IPT) version R2014a or later
- (OPTIONAL[1]) One or more of your images

Steps (Preparation)

1. Select and open the input image.
2. Apply desired geometric transformation to the image using a MATLAB function from Table 5.1.
3. (OPTIONAL) Display original and transformed images.
4. (OPTIONAL) Save the transformed image in any file format supported by MATLAB.

TABLE 5.1

Selected geometric operations available in MATLAB.

MATLAB function	Operation
imresize	resizing/scaling
imrotate	rotation
imtranslate	translation
imcrop	cropping

Examples

Part 1: Image resizing

Listing 5.1 shows an example of image resizing. In this particular case, the original image has been resized to 80% of its original size, from $972 \times 1296 \times 3$ to $778 \times 1037 \times 3$. The results are shown in Figure 5.1.

LISTING 5.1
Image resizing.

```
1 % Image resizing
2 img_1 = imread('flamingos.jpg');
3 img_2 = imresize(img_1, 0.8, "Method", "bicubic", "Antialiasing",true);
4 imshowpair(img_1, img_2, 'montage')
5 sz_img_1 = size(img_1);
6 sz_img_2 = size(img_2);
```

A common mistake that you should try to avoid when resizing an image is to specify a desired target size – in pixels – whose aspect ratio is different

FIGURE 5.1
Image resizing example. Original image: courtesy of The MathWorks.

FIGURE 5.2
Image resizing with incorrect specification of target image size. Original image: courtesy of The MathWorks.

FIGURE 5.3
Image resizing with correct specification of target image size. Original image: courtesy of The MathWorks.

from the original image. See Listing 5.2 and Figure 5.2 for an example of what **not** to do.

LISTING 5.2
Image resizing with wrong aspect ratio.

```
% Image resizing (wrong aspect ratio!)
img_1 = imread('flamingos.jpg');
img_2 = imresize(img_1, [1040 480]);
imshowpair(img_1, img_2, 'montage')
sz_img_1 = size(img_1);
sz_img_2 = size(img_2);
```

Fortunately, MATLAB provides an elegant solution to resize an image specifying either the number of rows or columns of the desired target size and leaving the other dimension as NaN, which preserves the aspect ratio of the original image. See Listing 5.3 and Figure 5.3.

FIGURE 5.4
Image rotation example. Original image: courtesy of The MathWorks.

LISTING 5.3
Image resizing while keeping the aspect ratio.

```
% Image resizing (preserving the correct aspect ratio)
img_1 = imread('flamingos.jpg');
img_2 = imresize(img_1, [NaN 480]); % We want 480 columns
imshowpair(img_1, img_2, 'montage')
sz_img_1 = size(img_1); % 972-by-1296 pixels
sz_img_2 = size(img_2); % 360-by-480 pixels
```

Part 2: Image rotation

Listing 5.4 shows an example of image rotation. In this particular case, the image is rotated counterclockwise by 35°. The results are shown in Figure 5.4.

LISTING 5.4
Image rotation.

```
% Image rotation
img_1 = imread('car1.jpg');
img_2 = imrotate(img_1, 35, "bicubic");
imshowpair(img_1, img_2, 'montage')
sz_img_1 = size(img_1);
sz_img_2 = size(img_2);
```

Note that when you rotate an image by an angle that is not a multiple of 90°, the resulting image will usually change size[2] to accommodate all the original pixels; the remaining pixels in the output image will be set to 0 by default. If you want the output image to be the same size as the input image (with the associated loss of contents), you can use the 'crop' option. See Listing 5.5 and Figure 5.5.

FIGURE 5.5
Image rotation with cropped output. Original image: courtesy of The MathWorks.

LISTING 5.5
Image rotation with cropped output.

```
% Image rotation (with cropped output)
img_1 = imread('car1.jpg');
img_2 = imrotate(img_1, 35, "bicubic","crop");
imshowpair(img_1, img_2, 'montage')
sz_img_1 = size(img_1);
sz_img_2 = size(img_2);
```

Part 3: Image translation

Listing 5.6 shows an example of image translation by 750 pixels down and 400 pixels to the right of the original coordinates. Note that when you translate an image, the resulting image will change size[3] to accommodate all the original pixels; the remaining pixels in the output image will be set to the value specified under the 'FillValues' option, which in this example was set to 255 (white). The results are shown in Figure 5.6.

LISTING 5.6
Image translation.

```
% Image translation
img_1 = imread('car2.jpg');
img_2 = imtranslate(img_1,[400, 750],'FillValues',255,'OutputView','full');
figure, imshow(img_1), title('Original Image'), ...
    set(gca,'Visible','on');
figure, imshow(img_2), title('Full Translated Image'), ...
    set(gca,'Visible','on');
sz_img_1 = size(img_1);
sz_img_2 = size(img_2);
```

If you want the output image to be of the same size as the input image (with the associated loss of contents), you can set the 'OutputView' option to 'Same'. See Listing 5.7 and Figure 5.7.

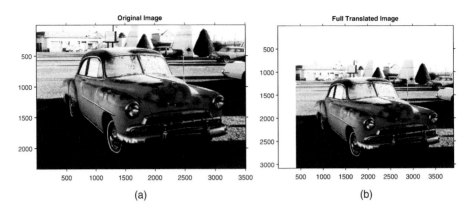

(a)   (b)

FIGURE 5.6
Image translation example. Original image: courtesy of The MathWorks.

(a)   (b)

FIGURE 5.7
Image translation with cropped output. Original image: courtesy of The MathWorks.

LISTING 5.7
Image translation with cropped output.

```
% Image translation (with cropped output)
img_1 = imread('car2.jpg');
img_2 = imtranslate(img_1,[400, 750],'FillValues',255,'OutputView','same');
figure, imshow(img_1), title('Original Image'), ...
    set(gca,'Visible','on');
figure, imshow(img_2), title('Full Translated Image'), ...
    set(gca,'Visible','on');
sz_img_1 = size(img_1);
sz_img_2 = size(img_2);
```

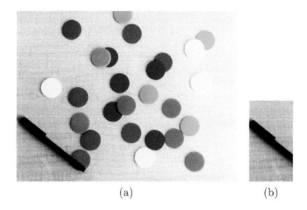

(a) (b)

FIGURE 5.8
Image cropping example. Original image: courtesy of The MathWorks.

Part 4: Image cropping

Listing 5.8 shows an example of image cropping, where the input image is cropped according to the position and dimensions specified in the crop rectangle 'rect'. The results are shown in Figure 5.8. The size of the original image is $391 \times 518 \times 3$ whereas the size of the cropped image is $181 \times 101 \times 3$.

LISTING 5.8
Image cropping (programmatic).

```
% Image cropping (programmatic)
img_1 = imread('coloredChips.png');
sz_img_1 = size(img_1);
rect = [10 200 100 180];
img_2 = imcrop(img_1, rect);
imshowpair(img_1, img_2, 'montage')
sz_img_2 = size(img_2);
```

Image cropping is often done interactively. In the example below (Figure 5.9 and Listing 5.9), we selected a small area containing the red circle closest to the top-left corner of the original image, resulting in a rectangle 'rect' whose values are: [82.5100 5.5100 90.9800 76.9800]. Note that between lines 4 and 5, MATLAB enters the interactive mode where the program execution is temporarily stopped, and the user is expected to use the mouse to define the cropping rectangle. Once a region has been selected, the remaining lines in the script are then executed. The size of the original image is $391 \times 518 \times 3$ whereas the size of the cropped image is $77 \times 91 \times 3$.

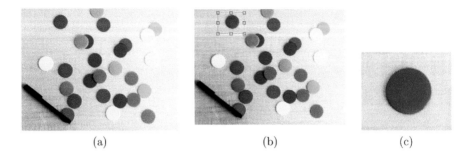

FIGURE 5.9
Image cropping example: (a) input image; (b) interactive selection of desired cropped area; (c) resulting (cropped) image. Original image: courtesy of The MathWorks.

LISTING 5.9
Image cropping (interactive).

```
% Image cropping (interactive)
img_1 = imread('coloredChips.png');
sz_img_1 = size(img_1);
[img_2, rect] = imcrop(img_1); %interactive cropping
imwrite(img_2,'cropped_image.png');
imshowpair(img_1, img_2, 'montage')
sz_img_2 = size(img_2);
```

Discussion (Recipe notes)

In this recipe, you learned how to apply fundamental geometric transformations to images using MATLAB built-in functions (Table 5.1).

The syntax used for each example illustrates one of many possible uses of each associated library function. You are encouraged to expand upon each example in this recipe, particularly:

- For `imresize`: try other magnification factors, interpolation methods, and options.
- For `imrotate`: try other rotation angles, interpolation methods, and options.
- For `imtranslate`: try other fill values, interpolation methods, and options.
- For `imcrop`: try other image types (including indexed color images) and options.

In Recipe 6, we will expand upon this topic and teach you how to perform image warping and other geometric operations.

Learn more about it

Useful MATLAB functions

Type the function name in the search field at www.mathworks.com/help/matlab/
· imcrop · imresize · imrotate · imtranslate ·

MATLAB documentation, demos, and examples

- Common Geometric Transformations
  www.mathworks.com/help/images/geometric-transformations.html
- Crop an Image
  www.mathworks.com/help/images/crop-an-image.html
- Resize an Image
  www.mathworks.com/help/images/resize-an-image.html
- Resize Image and Preserve Aspect Ratio
  www.mathworks.com/help/images/resize-image-and-preserve-aspect-ratio.html
- Rotate an Image
  www.mathworks.com/help/images/rotate-an-image.html
- Translate an Image Using imtranslate Function
  www.mathworks.com/help/images/translate-an-image.html

Notes

1 The recipe has been prepared using MATLAB's built-in images.
2 In this particular case, the image size will change from $2336 \times 3504 \times 3$ to $3924 \times 4211 \times 3$.
3 In this particular case, the image size will change from $2336 \times 3504 \times 3$ to $3086 \times 3904 \times 3$.

6

Recipe 6: Image warping

This recipe teaches you how to create affine transformations specifying arbitrary geometric operations and apply them to images.

In Recipe 5, you learned how to perform some of the most frequently used geometric transformations to 2D images using MATLAB's built-in functions for image resizing, cropping, rotation, and translation. In this recipe, you'll learn how to apply *any* 2D affine geometric transformation using MATLAB. To better understand what affine transformations are, here is a summary of the theory.

A geometric operation can be described mathematically as the process of transforming an input image $f(x, y)$ into a new image $g(x', y')$ by modifying the *coordinates* of image pixels:

$$f(x, y) \rightarrow g(x', y') \tag{6.1}$$

i.e., the pixel value originally located at coordinates (x, y) will be relocated to coordinates (x', y') in the output image.

To model this process, a *mapping function* is needed. The mapping function specifies the new coordinates (in the output image) for each pixel in the input image:

$$(x', y') = T(x, y) \tag{6.2}$$

This mapping function is an arbitrary 2D function. It is often specified as two separate functions, one for each dimension:

$$x' = T_x(x, y) \tag{6.3}$$

and

$$y' = T_y(x, y). \tag{6.4}$$

where T_x and T_y are usually expressed as polynomials in x and y. The case where T_x and T_y are linear combinations of x and y is called *affine transformation* (or *affine mapping*):

DOI: 10.1201/9781003170198-8

TABLE 6.1

Summary of transformation coefficients for selected affine transformations.

Transformation	a_0	a_1	a_2	b_0	b_1	b_2
Translation by Δ_x, Δ_y	1	0	Δ_x	0	1	Δ_y
Scaling by a factor $[s_x, s_y]$	s_x	0	0	0	s_y	0
Counterclockwise rotation by angle θ	$\cos\theta$	$\sin\theta$	0	$-\sin\theta$	$\cos\theta$	0
Shear by a factor $[sh_x, sh_y]$	1	sh_x	0	sh_y	1	0

$$x' = a_0 x + a_1 y + a_2, \tag{6.5}$$

$$y' = b_0 x + b_1 y + b_2. \tag{6.6}$$

Equations 6.5 and 6.6 can also be expressed in matrix form as:

$$\begin{bmatrix} x' \\ y' \\ 1 \end{bmatrix} = \begin{bmatrix} a_0 & a_1 & a_2 \\ b_0 & b_1 & b_2 \\ 0 & 0 & 1 \end{bmatrix} \begin{bmatrix} x \\ y \\ 1 \end{bmatrix} \tag{6.7}$$

Affine mapping transforms straight lines to straight lines, triangles to triangles, and rectangles to parallelograms. Parallel lines remain parallel, and the distance ratio between points on a straight line does not change. Four of the most common geometric operations – translation, scaling (resizing), rotation, and shearing – are all special cases of Equation 6.7, as summarized in Table 6.1.

In MATLAB, you will use `affinetform2d` to store information about a 2D affine geometric transformation and `imwarp` to apply the selected transformation to an image.

You will need (Ingredients)

- MATLAB R2022b or later
- MATLAB Image Processing Toolbox (IPT) version R2022b or later
- (OPTIONAL[1]) One or more of your images

Steps (Preparation)

1. Select and open the input image.
2. Specify desired 2D affine transformation using `affinetform2d`.
3. Apply desired geometric transformation to the image using `imwarp`.

4. (OPTIONAL) Display original and transformed images.

5. (OPTIONAL) Save the transformed image in any file format supported by MATLAB.

Examples

Part 1: Image resizing

Listing 6.1 shows an example of image resizing (to 80% of its original size, from $972 \times 1296 \times 3$ to $778 \times 1037 \times 3$). The results are shown in Figure 6.1 and are identical to the ones in Figure 5.1 (Recipe 5).

LISTING 6.1
Image scaling using 2D affine transformation.

```
% Image scaling using 2D affine transformation
img_1 = imread('flamingos.jpg');
sz_img_1 = size(img_1);
affine_transform_1 = affinetform2d([.8 0 0; 0 .8 0; 0 0 1]);
img_2 = imwarp(img_1,affine_transform_1);
imshowpair(img_1, img_2, 'montage')
sz_img_2 = size(img_2);
```

Part 2: Image rotation

Listing 6.2 shows an example of image rotation (counterclockwise, by 35°). The results are shown in Figure 6.2 and are identical to the ones in Figure 5.4 (Recipe 5).

FIGURE 6.1
Image resizing example. Original image: courtesy of The MathWorks.

FIGURE 6.2
Image rotation example. Original image: courtesy of The MathWorks.

LISTING 6.2
Image rotation using 2D affine transformation.

```
% Image rotation using 2D affine transformation
img_1 = imread('car1.jpg');
sz_img_1 = size(img_1);
rotation_angle = 35; % in degrees
sin_ra = sind(rotation_angle);
cos_ra = cosd(rotation_angle);
affine_transform_2 = affinetform2d([cos_ra sin_ra 0; -sin_ra cos_ra 0; 0 0 1]);
img_2 = imwarp(img_1,affine_transform_2);
imshowpair(img_1, img_2, 'montage')
sz_img_2 = size(img_2);
```

Part 3: Image shearing

The greater flexibility of using 2D affine transforms with arbitrary coefficients allows the use of geometric transformations (distortions) that could not be implemented (with simpler syntax and fewer steps) using the built-in functions from Recipe 5. One example of such distortions is the *shearing* operation, which shifts one part of an image in a specific direction and the other in the opposite direction.

Listing 6.3 shows an example of image shearing. The results are shown in Figure 6.3. Note that the resulting image will change size (in this case, from $2336 \times 3504 \times 3$ to $2336 \times 4672 \times 3$) to accommodate all the original pixels; the remaining pixels in the output image will be set to 0 (black).

FIGURE 6.3

Image shearing example. Original image: courtesy of The MathWorks.

LISTING 6.3

Image shearing using 2D affine transformation.

```
% Image shearing using 2D affine transformation
img_1 = imread('car2.jpg');
% Define 2D affine transform
coefficients = [1 0.5 0; 0 1 0; 0 0 1];
affine_transform_3 = affinetform2d(coefficients);
% Apply transform
img_2 = imwarp(img_1,affine_transform_3);
% View results
imshowpair(img_1, img_2, 'montage')
sz_img_1 = size(img_1);
sz_img_2 = size(img_2);
```

Part 4: Combining multiple distortions

Affine transformations can be encapsulated using the `randomAffine2d`, which can be helpful in the context of image data augmentation for deep learning solutions in computer vision.

Listing 6.4 shows an example of using `randomAffine2d` with fixed values for `Scale`, `XShear`, `YShear`, and `Rotation`. The results are shown in Figure 6.4. As expected, the resulting image is larger, sheared, and rotated. In case you're curious, behind the scenes `randomAffine2d` created a 3×3 matrix (see Equation 6.7) whose coefficients are: $a_0 = 0.4823$, $b_0 = -1.8000$, $a_1 = 1.8000$, and $b_1 = -0.3174$. Since no translation is involved, both a_2 and b_2 are equal to zero.

LISTING 6.4

Combining 2D affine transformations.

```
% Combining several 2D affine transformations
img_1 = imread('football.jpg');
% Define 2D affine transform
affine_transform_4 = randomAffine2d('Scale',[1.8 1.8], ...
    'XShear',[10 10], 'YShear', [15 15], ...
    'Rotation',[90 90]);
% Apply transform
img_2 = imwarp(img_1,affine_transform_4);
% View results
imshowpair(img_1, img_2, 'montage')
sz_img_1 = size(img_1);
sz_img_2 = size(img_2);
```

FIGURE 6.4
Combining multiple distortions in one pass. Original image: courtesy of The MathWorks.

Discussion (Recipe notes)

In this recipe, you learned how to apply geometric transformations to images using MATLAB built-in functions affinetform2d and imwarp. You also learned to combine multiple geometric transformations in one line of code using randomaffine2d.

Admittedly, we have just scratched the surface of the vast area of designing and applying geometric distortions to images. You are encouraged to modify and expand the examples to your specific needs. See the links below for ideas.

Learn more about it

Useful MATLAB functions

Type the function name in the search field at www.mathworks.com/help/matlab/
· affinetform2d · imwarp · randomaffine2d ·

MATLAB documentation, demos, and examples

- 2-D and 3-D Geometric Transformation Process Overview
  www.mathworks.com/help/images/2-d-and-3-d-geometric-transformation-process-overview.html

- Create Composite 2-D Affine Transformations
  `www.mathworks.com/help/images/create-composite-2d-affine-transf`
  `ormation.html`
- Create a Gallery of Transformed Images
  `www.mathworks.com/help/images/creating-a-gallery-of-transformed`
  `-images.html`
- Matrix Representation of Geometric Transformations
  `www.mathworks.com/help/images/matrix-representation-of-geometri`
  `c-transformations.html`
- Perform Simple 2-D Translation Transformation
  `www.mathworks.com/help/images/perform-a-2-d-translation-transf`
  `ormation.html`

Note

1   The recipe has been prepared using MATLAB's built-in images.

Part III

Histograms

Part III – Histograms

This Part contains recipes that focus on histogram-based image processing techniques. Histograms are a convenient way to summarize the distribution of an image's intensity (or color) values. You will learn how to compute, display, interpret, modify, and explore the histograms of grayscale and color images.

Recipe 7 shows how to compute and display histograms and statistics of grayscale images.

Recipe 8 helps you expand upon that knowledge and perform contrast and intensity adjustments on images using histogram-based techniques.

Recipe 9 shifts our attention from grayscale to color images and teaches you how to compute and display the histograms of individual color channels of color images.

Recipe 10 teaches you how to quantize the colors in an image, compute and display the resulting histogram, and obtain the dominant colors of the image.

DOI: 10.1201/9781003170198-9

7

Recipe 7: Histograms and statistics of grayscale images

This recipe teaches you how to compute and display histograms and statistics of grayscale images.

You will need (Ingredients)

- MATLAB R2019b or later
- MATLAB Image Processing Toolbox (IPT) version R2019b or later
- (OPTIONAL[1]) One or more of your own images

Steps (Preparation)

1. Select and open the input image.
2. Compute and display the corresponding histogram.
3. (OPTIONAL) Compute and display relevant summary statistics about the image's pixel contents.
4. (OPTIONAL) Save histogram plot in any file format supported by MATLAB.

Part 1: Basic histogram display

Listing 7.1 uses the `imhist` function to compute and display the histogram of an image (see results in Figure 7.1).

LISTING 7.1
Histogram of a grayscale image.

```
% Histograms - grayscale images
img_1 = imread('circuit.tif');
figure
subplot(2,1,1), imshow(img_1), title('Image')
subplot(2,1,2), imhist(img_1,256), title('Histogram')
```

Image

Histogram

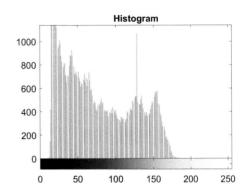

FIGURE 7.1
An image and its histogram. Original image: courtesy of The MathWorks.

Part 2: Improved histogram display

The default options for displaying a histogram using `imhist` are convenient for a quick display of the image's histogram. A closer inspection, however, reveals that there are at least four aspects over which you might want to have greater control:

1. Use a different number of bins.
2. Adjust the height of the bars to prevent any bars whose height is greater than the vertical dimension of the plot from being clipped.
3. Use more flexible plot options (e.g., colors and markers).
4. Store the histogram counts for further processing.

Listing 7.2 addresses the first issue by specifying different values for the number of bins as a second parameter to `imhist`. Histograms tend to become less useful when the number of bins is lower than a certain threshold (which varies from one case to the next), as you can see in Figure 7.2.

LISTING 7.2
Histograms with different numbers of bins.

```
% Histograms with different numbers of bins
img_1 = imread('circuit.tif');
figure
subplot(3,1,1), imhist(img_1,256), title('Histogram with 256 bins')
subplot(3,1,2), imhist(img_1,64), title('Histogram with 64 bins')
subplot(3,1,3), imhist(img_1,16), title('Histogram with 16 bins')
```

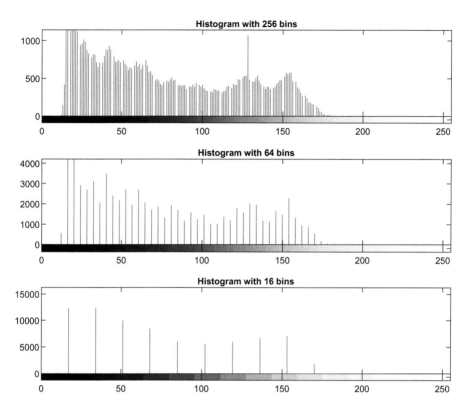

FIGURE 7.2
Varying the number of bins used to display the histogram of the image at the left of Figure 7.1.

Listing 7.3 addresses the three remaining issues. It illustrates how to store the histogram counts for further processing (e.g., converting absolute counts into percentages) and uses the `stem` function for greater flexibility regarding the histogram's visual aspects[2]. We also introduce the `tiledlayout` function and use it to create a 2-by-1 `TiledChartLayout` object that manages the display of the image and its histogram into the `figure` (Figure 7.3). Lines 8–10 will produce the following messages on the command window:

```
The tallest peak (at gray level 73) corresponds to 5.78 %
of the pixels in the image

Pixel percentages add up to 1.000000
```

Image

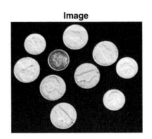

Histogram

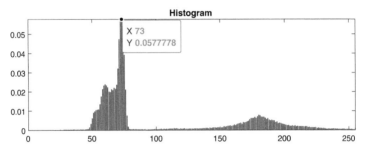

FIGURE 7.3
Using the stem function to display the histogram of an image with greater control over the appearance of the histogram. Original image: courtesy of The MathWorks.

LISTING 7.3
Histograms using stem.

```
% Histograms using stem
img_1 = imread('coins.png');

[pixel_counts, gray_levels] = imhist(img_1,256);
pixel_percentages = pixel_counts / numel(img_1);
[max_percent, idx_max_percent] = max(pixel_percentages);

fprintf(['The tallest peak (at gray level %d) corresponds to %.2f %%' ...
    ' of the pixels in the image \n'], idx_max_percent-1, 100*max_percent);
fprintf('Pixel percentages add up to %f', sum(pixel_percentages));

figure
t = tiledlayout(2,1);
t.TileSpacing = 'tight'; t.Padding = 'compact';
nexttile, imshow(img_1), title('Image')
nexttile, stem(0:255, pixel_percentages, 'Marker','none', ...
    'Color','#CC33BB', 'LineWidth',1)
set(gca,'ylim',[0 max_percent],'xlim',[0 255]), title('Histogram')
```

Discussion (Recipe notes)

In this recipe you learned how to compute, display, and explore the contents of histograms of grayscale images.

You are encouraged to expand upon each example in this recipe, particularly:

- Explore additional options associated with the `stem` function and other plotting capabilities in MATLAB.
- Play with the `histogram` function and see whether its functionality overlaps with `stem` and `imhist`.
- Explore histogram values (counts and associated percentages) further, e.g., computing useful summary statistics (mean, median, max, min, standard deviation, etc.) for each image, i.e., treating a histogram as a probability mass function (PMF) of gray levels (which can be thought of as discrete random variables whose values lie between 0 and 255) in the image.

Learn more about it

Useful MATLAB functions

Type the function name in the search field at www.mathworks.com/help/matlab/

· `histogram` · `imhist` · `stem` ·

MATLAB documentation, demos, and examples

- Create Image Histogram
  www.mathworks.com/help/images/create-image-histogram.html
- Working with Probability Distributions
  www.mathworks.com/help/stats/working-with-probability-distributions.html

Notes

1   The recipe has been prepared using MATLAB's built-in images.
2   Note how we had to reconcile MATLAB's 1-based array indexing with the fact that gray levels vary from 0 to 255 (line 9 in the code).

8

Recipe 8: Histogram equalization and histogram matching

This recipe teaches you how to perform contrast and intensity adjustments on images using two popular histogram-based techniques: histogram equalization and histogram matching.

You will need (Ingredients)

- MATLAB R2012b or later
- MATLAB Image Processing Toolbox (IPT) version R2012b or later
- (OPTIONAL[1]) One or more of your images

Steps (Preparation)

1. Select and open the input image.
2. (OPTIONAL) Compute and display its histogram.
3. Perform histogram equalization (or matching) using the appropriate library function(s).
4. Display the processed image (and associated histogram) and assess the results.
5. (OPTIONAL) Save/export resulting figures and images using any file format supported by MATLAB.

Part 1: Histogram equalization

Histogram equalization is a technique that rearranges the distribution of pixel values in a grayscale image to produce a uniform histogram, in which (ideally[2]) the percentage of pixels of every gray level is the same. The basic histogram equalization technique (available in MATLAB as `histeq`) can be

        DOI: 10.1201/9781003170198-11

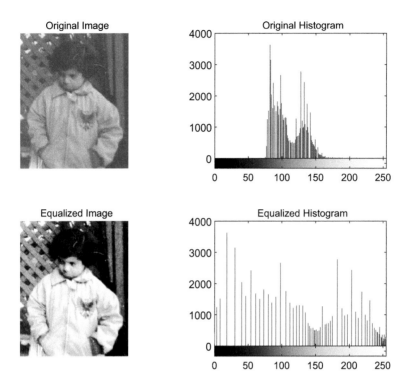

FIGURE 8.1
An image and its histogram, before and after histogram equalization. Original image: courtesy of The MathWorks.

used as a contrast enhancement algorithm when the original image's gray levels are grouped in a narrow range of gray levels.

See Figure 8.1 to compare the results *before* and *after* the histogram equalization operation using the code in Listing 8.1. In this particular case, you will probably agree that the image quality was enhanced as a result of applying this technique.

LISTING 8.1
Histogram equalization.

```
% Histogram equalization
img_1 = imread('pout.tif');
img_1_eq = histeq(img_1,256);
figure
subplot(2,2,1), imshow(img_1), title('Original Image')
subplot(2,2,2), imhist(img_1), ylim('auto'), title('Original Histogram')
subplot(2,2,3), imshow(img_1_eq), title('Equalized Image')
subplot(2,2,4), imhist(img_1_eq), ylim('auto'), title('Equalized Histogram')
```

The basic histogram equalization algorithm implemented by `his-teq` has inherent limitations. An improved version of `histeq`, called `adapthisteq`, implements the Contrast-Limited Adaptive Histogram Equalization (CLAHE) algorithm [26]. CLAHE operates on small regions in the image, called *tiles*, rather than the entire image. The `adapthisteq` function calculates the contrast transform function for each tile individually, and neighboring tiles are combined using bilinear interpolation to eliminate artificially induced boundaries.

See Figure 8.2 to compare the results *before* and *after* the histogram equalization operation for both `histeq` (middle row) and `adapthisteq` (bottom row) using the code in Listing 8.2. You will probably agree that – for this particular image – the results obtained using CLAHE are far superior.

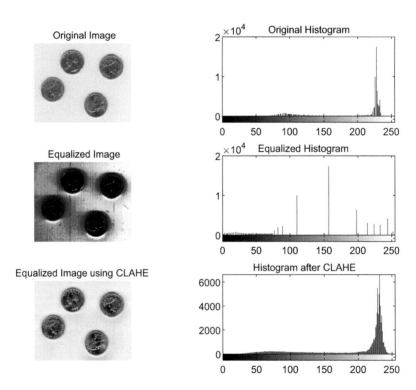

FIGURE 8.2
Adaptive histogram equalization. Original image: courtesy of The MathWorks.

LISTING 8.2
Histogram equalization using CLAHE.

```
% Histogram equalization using CLAHE
img_1 = imread('eight.tif');
img_1_eq = histeq(img_1,256);
img_1_clahe_eq = adapthisteq(img_1);
subplot(3,2,1), imshow(img_1), title('Original Image')
subplot(3,2,2), imhist(img_1), ylim('auto'), title('Original Histogram')
subplot(3,2,3), imshow(img_1_eq), title('Equalized Image')
subplot(3,2,4), imhist(img_1_eq), ylim('auto'), ...
    title('Equalized Histogram')
subplot(3,2,5), imshow(img_1_clahe_eq), ...
    title('Equalized Image using CLAHE')
subplot(3,2,6), imhist(img_1_clahe_eq), ylim('auto'), ...
    title('Histogram after CLAHE')
```

Part 2: Histogram matching

Despite its usefulness in contrast enhancement, histogram equalization has some limitations. For example, there are situations in which you want to be able to perform *specific* changes on the original histogram, e.g., to make it match – as closely as possible – another image's histogram. In these situations, a helpful technique is the *direct histogram specification*, also known as *histogram matching*.

In MATLAB, histogram matching can be implemented using the imhistmatch function. Listing 8.3 shows how it can be used to adjust the histogram of a 2D image to match the histogram of a *reference image*. Results are shown in Figure 8.3. Note how the histogram on the bottom-right portion of the figure is much closer to the histogram of the reference image (middle row) than the histogram of the original image (top row).

LISTING 8.3
Histogram matching.

```
% Histogram matching
img_1 = imread('pout.tif'); % Original image
ref_img = imread('coins.png'); % Reference image
matched_img = imhistmatch(img_1, ref_img);

subplot(3,2,1), imshow(img_1), title('Original Image')
subplot(3,2,2), imhist(img_1), ylim('auto'), ...
    title('Histogram of Original Image')
subplot(3,2,3), imshow(ref_img), title('Reference Image')
subplot(3,2,4), imhist(ref_img), ylim('auto'), ...
    title(' Histogram of Reference Image')
subplot(3,2,5), imshow(matched_img), ...
    title('Histogram matched image')
subplot(3,2,6), imhist(matched_img), ylim('auto'), ...
    title('Modified Histogram')
```

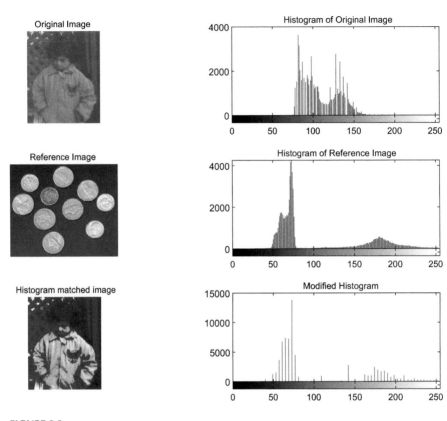

FIGURE 8.3
Histogram matching. Original image: courtesy of The MathWorks.

Discussion (Recipe notes)

In this recipe, you learned how to perform histogram equalization and histogram matching. Our examples used grayscale images for the sake of simplicity.

You are encouraged to expand upon each example in this recipe, particularly:

- Extend the examples to include color images and image stacks (e.g., MRI slices).
- Explore additional options associated with the imhistmatch function. Check the official documentation for ideas.

Learn more about it

Useful MATLAB functions

Type the function name in the search field at www.mathworks.com/help/matlab/
· adapthisteq · histeq · imhistmatch · stretchlim ·

MATLAB documentation, demos, and examples

- Adaptive Histogram Equalization
  www.mathworks.com/help/images/adaptive-histogram-equalization.html

- Adjust Image Contrast Using Histogram Equalization
  www.mathworks.com/help/images/histogram-equalization.html

- Contrast Enhancement Techniques
  www.mathworks.com/help/images/contrast-enhancement-techniques.html

Notes

1 The recipe has been prepared using MATLAB's built-in images.
2 Since we are dealing with digital images, this is usually not possible and we have to settle for a resulting histogram that is "as close to a uniform distribution as it can get."

9

Recipe 9: Individual channel histograms of color images

This recipe teaches you how to compute and display the histograms of individual color channels of color images.

You will need (Ingredients)

- MATLAB R2019b or later
- MATLAB Image Processing Toolbox (IPT) version R2019b or later
- (OPTIONAL[1]) One or more of your images

Steps (Preparation)

1. Load input image.
2. (OPTIONAL) Convert the image to another color model.
3. Select the channel(s) of interest – e.g., for RGB images, you'll probably want the individual color channels (*R, G, and B*), whereas, for images in the YIQ color space, you'll probably choose the luminance (Y) of the image.
4. Compute the histogram of the desired channels using `imhist`.
5. Display the histogram(s) using `imhist` or `stem`.

Part 1: Histograms of individual color channels of an RGB image

Color images can be represented in different *color models*, also named *color spaces*[2]. In the RGB color space, each pixel is expressed as a combination of the three primary (component) colors, one per channel – red (R), green (G), and blue (B). RGB color images are usually encoded using 24 bits per pixel,

            DOI: 10.1201/9781003170198-12

i.e., 8 bits per pixel in each channel, and are called *true color* images. Considering the available combinations of *R, G, and B,* each in the range [0, 255], a true color image allows for the representation of $256 \times 256 \times 256 = 16,777,216$ distinct colors.

Since histograms comprising this large number of colors would not be practical (or meaningful), a possible approach is to show each color channel individually.

The code in Listing 9.1 displays, in a single MATLAB `figure`, the input color image, its *R, G, and B* channels as intensity images, and the respective histograms. The input is a true color image, assigned to the RGB multidimensional array $M \times N \times 3$, where M is the number of rows and N is the number of columns. The commands R = RGB(:,:,1); G = RGB(:,:,2); B = RGB(:,:,3); decompose the image into individual color channels and their respective histograms are computed with the `imhist` function. The `countMax` variable stores the maximum pixel count among the three histograms to adjust the y axis of the histograms and plot them at the same scale. The `tiledlayout` function creates a 3-by-3 `TiledChartLayout` object that manages the display of the images and histograms into the `figure`. The `nexttile([3 1])` function spans one display region to 3-by-1, which is used to show the input image. To plot the histogram, we use the `stem` function, a versatile option to present images' histograms[3].

LISTING 9.1
Histograms of individual color channels of RGB images.

```
 1  % Histograms of individual color channels of RGB images
 2  img = imread('lighthouse.png');
 3  %img = imread('fabric.png');
 4
 5  img_r = img(:,:,1); img_g = img(:,:,2); img_b = img(:,:,3);
 6  hist_r = imhist(img_r); hist_g = imhist(img_g); hist_b = imhist(img_b);
 7  count_max = max([hist_r; hist_g; img_bh]);
 8
 9  figure
10  t = tiledlayout(3,3);
11  t.TileSpacing = 'tight'; t.Padding = 'compact';
12
13  nexttile([3 1]), imshow(img)
14  nexttile, imshow(img_r)
15  nexttile, stem(0:255,hist_r,'Marker','none','Color','r','LineWidth',1)
16  set(gca,'ylim',[0 count_max],'xlim',[0 255],'xticklabels',[])
17  nexttile, imshow(img_g)
18  nexttile, stem(0:255,hist_g,'Marker','none','Color','g','LineWidth',1)
19  set(gca,'ylim',[0 count_max],'xlim',[0 255],'xticklabels',[])
20  nexttile, imshow(img_b)
21  nexttile, stem(0:255,hist_b,'Marker','none','Color','b','LineWidth',1)
22  set(gca,'ylim',[0 count_max],'xlim',[0 255])
```

Figure 9.1 presents the output of the code for the `fabric.png` and `lighthouse.png` built-in images.

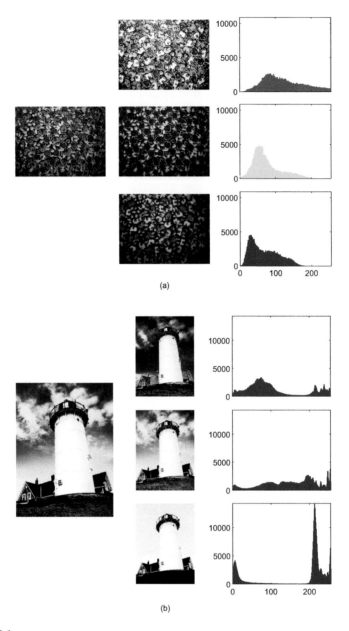

(a)

(b)

FIGURE 9.1

Results of decomposing a true color RGB image into its individual channels and computing the respective histograms (see Listing 9.1). The input image is shown at the left, and the *R, G, and B* channels, from top to bottom, as intensity images. (a) The histogram of the R channel presents a large bin at the 255 value, demonstrating that many pixels of the image have saturated R values. (b) The histogram of the B channel presents a peak between 200 and 225 due to the bluish pixels of the sky in the image and many of the whitish pixels. Original images: courtesy of The MathWorks.

Part 2: Histogram of the luminance component of a color image

Another possibility is to compute the histogram of the "grayscale version" of the color image. This can be accomplished using a conversion from RGB to a color space that separates the *chroma* components (color information) from the *luminance* (achromatic information) of the image. The YIQ color space, for example, employs this method – Y is the luminance, while I and Q encode the chromaticity of the image.

In Listing 9.2, built-in images `office_5.jpg` and `office_6.jpg` are converted from RGB to YIQ by the `rgb2ntsc` function, then the respective Y channels are isolated, and their histograms are computed and displayed by `imhist` function. Figure 9.2 shows the results.

LISTING 9.2
Histogram of the luminance component of a color image.

```
% Histogram of the luminance component of a color image
img_1 = imread('office_5.jpg');
img_2 = imread('office_6.jpg');

img_1_yiq  = rgb2ntsc(img_1); img_2_yiq = rgb2ntsc(img_2);
img_1_y = im2uint8(img_1_yiq(:,:,1)); img_2_y = im2uint8(img_2_yiq(:,:,1));

figure
subplot(2,3,1), imshow(img_1), title('Image 1')
subplot(2,3,2), imshow(img_1_y), title('Y')
subplot(2,3,3), imhist(img_1_y), axis tight
subplot(2,3,4), imshow(img_2), title('Image 2')
subplot(2,3,5), imshow(img_2_y), title('Y')
subplot(2,3,6), imhist(img_2_y), axis tight
```

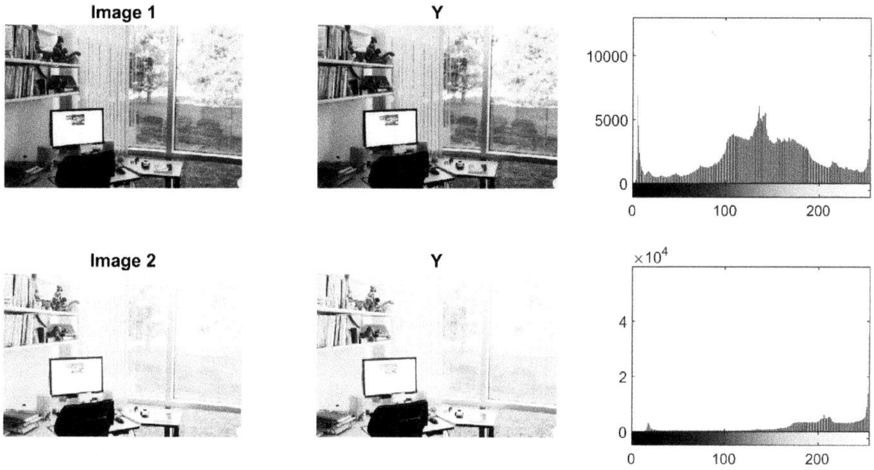

FIGURE 9.2
Output of the code to display the histogram of the luminance of two color images. From left to right: the original color images, their Y (luminance) channels obtained using an RGB to YIQ color space conversion, and the histograms. Histograms show that *Image 2* is considerably more saturated with light pixels than *Image 1*. Original images: courtesy of The MathWorks.

Discussion (Recipe notes)

In this recipe, you learned how to compute and display individual channel histograms of color images.

Although individual channel histograms of color images may convey helpful information, as demonstrated in the examples in this recipe, they do not summarize the combination of the channels into an image. You will learn how to compute and display combined color histograms in Recipe 10.

Learn more about it

Useful MATLAB functions

Type the function name in the search field at www.mathworks.com/help/matlab/

· imhist · rgb2ntsc · stem · tiledlayout ·

MATLAB documentation, demos, and examples

- Understanding Color Spaces and Color Space Conversion
  www.mathworks.com/help/images/understanding-color-spaces-and-color-space-conversion.html

Notes

1   The recipe has been prepared using MATLAB's built-in images.
2   You will learn more about color spaces in Recipe 26.
3   See Recipe 7.

10

Recipe 10: *Combined color histograms and dominant colors in an image*

This recipe teaches you how to reduce the number of colors in an image (a process known as *quantization*), compute and display the resultant histogram, and identify the dominant colors within the image.

You will need (Ingredients)

- MATLAB R2016b or later
- MATLAB Image Processing Toolbox (IPT) version R2016b or later
- (OPTIONAL[1]) One or more of your images

Steps (Preparation)

1. Load input image.
2. Reduce the number of colors of the image using a quantization, with `rgb2ind`.
3. Compute the histogram of the color quantized image using `imhist`.
4. Display the histogram(s) using `bar`.

Each pixel of a *true color* RGB image is expressed as a combination of the three primary (component) colors, one per channel – red (R), green (G), and blue (B). RGB color images are usually encoded using 24 bits per pixel, i.e., 8 bits per pixel in each channel, representing $256 \times 256 \times 256 = 16{,}777{,}216$ distinct colors. Even though a color image typically does not contain pixels with every color combination, it is common to find thousands of unique colors in a true color image.

As an example, we can find the unique colors of a built-in image by typing the following commands:

DOI: 10.1201/9781003170198-13

```
img = imread('flamingos.jpg');
[img_idx, img_cmap] = cmunique(img);
nuc = size(img_cmap,1)
```

The cmunique function converts the true color input image into a MAT-LAB *indexed image*, eliminating the duplicated colors present in the image. The outputs are a matrix img_idx of the same width and height of the input image and a colormap img_cmap containing the unique colors of the input image. Each pixel of img_idx contains the index of the row of img_cmap, which stores the pixel's R, G, and B values. In MATLAB, a *colormap* is a $N \times 3$ matrix, where N is the number of colors and the three columns consist of the values of R, G, B, in the [0, 1.0] range. The number of rows of the colormap in variable nuc corresponds to the number of unique colors of the images:

```
nuc =
    194001
```

We can use the opportunity to inspect an indexed color image using MATLAB's *Pixel Region* tool:

```
imshow(img_idx, img_cmap)
impixelregion
```

The outputs of these commands are shown in Figure 10.1. The impixelregion function displays a rectangle in the figure created by imshow (center of the cross in Figure 10.1(a)), and a new corresponding figure window, named *Pixel Region* (Figure 10.1(b)). You can change the position and the dimensions of the rectangle that inspects the image interactively using the mouse. Moreover, when the mouse cursor is positioned on the Pixel Region window, the coordinates and value of the pixel are presented at the *Pixel info* region, as shown in Figure 10.1(c).

To conclude our inspection of the elements of an indexed color image, type the following commands to access the image matrix img_idx, the colormap img_cmap, and confirm the values obtained with the *Pixel Region* tool, shown in Figure 10.1(c):

```
p = img_idx(486,648)
cmapRow = img_cmap(p,:)
```

As expected, we obtained the following:

```
p =
     81569
cmapRow =
    0.9609    0.4902    0.2861
```

Note that the *Pixel Region* tool specifies the pixel coordinates in (X, Y) notation (Figure 10.1(b)), and to access it the $(row, column)$ notation is required. Thus, in the code above, access to the pixel $X = 648$ and $Y = 486$ (Figure 10.1(c)) is specified as $(486, 648)$.

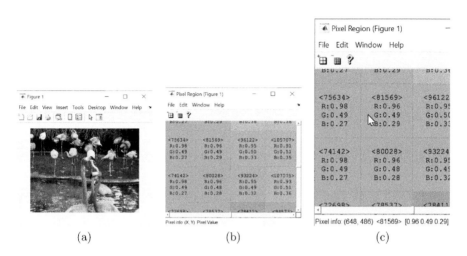

(a)   (b)   (c)

FIGURE 10.1
Inspection of a color image with the *Pixel Region* tool. (a) Image with the original colors. (b) The region corresponding to the small rectangle in (a); $< p >$ is the value into the image matrix and R, G, B the color into the colormap at row $< p >$. (c) Mouse pointer's *Pixel info*, in the bottom of the window. Original image: courtesy of The MathWorks.

It is possible to visualize all the colors present in an image using a *point cloud* representation, where each color is expressed as a point in the specified color space. In MATLAB, the `colorcloud` function provides a *Panel* object that shows the 3D color space and the distribution of the image's colors.

The following commands show MATLAB's color cloud for the built-in image `flamingos.jpg` in the RGB color space. Results are presented in Figure 10.2, where part (b) shows the distribution of the colors in the image (a) in the RGB color space, in the original view presented by `colorcloud` function, whereas part (c) presents a rotated[2] view, allowing the visualization of the colors mapping the green vegetation in the image.

```
img_1 = imread('flamingos.jpg');
colorcloud(img_1)
```

The code in Listing 10.1 shows MATLAB's color cloud for the built-in image `lighthouse.png` for both RGB and HSV color spaces. Figure 10.3 shows the results for the cube-shaped RGB color space (part (b)) and the HSV color space (part (c)), represented by an inverted cone.

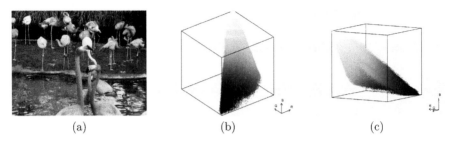

(a)   (b)   (c)

FIGURE 10.2
Visualization of the colors in an image with the `colorcloud` function. Original image: courtesy of The MathWorks.

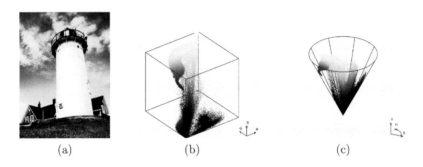

(a)   (b)   (c)

FIGURE 10.3
Visualization of the colors in an image with the `colorcloud` function. Original image: courtesy of The MathWorks.

LISTING 10.1
Visualization of the colors in different color spaces (RGB and HSV).

```
1  % Visualization of the colors in different color spaces
2  img_2 = imread('lighthouse.png');
3  figure, imshow(img_2)
4  colorcloud(img_2)
5  colorcloud(img_2,'hsv')
```

Color clouds provide a helpful way to visualize **all** the colors present in an image, but they cannot summarize the image's color contents. Conversely, a combined color histogram with thousands of colors – in this example, 194,001 different colors – is impractical. Thus, a *reduction of the number of colors* is required. This is obtained using *color quantization*.

The most straightforward color quantization method is the *uniform quantization*, in which each color channel is quantized using fixed-size ranges. Considering the RGB color space, performing uniform quantization results in partitioning the RGB cube into smaller cubes of the same size, and the obtained quantized colors are those of the center of the cubes. In this type of quantization, the actual colors present in the image are *not* taken into account to determine the partitions.

Color quantization methods that factor in the colors in the image are likely to produce better results. In MATLAB, such quantization can be achieved using the rgb2ind function, which uses a method called *minimum variance quantization*. In the context of the RGB color space, the results of this quantization process don't always yield uniform cubes; instead, they depend on the specific colors present in the image. The resulting quantized colors represent the center of these cubes.

Listing 10.2 shows code for performing color quantization using rgb2ind, followed by the computation and displaying of the respective histogram. The number of quantized colors is assigned to the variable n, and the rgb2ind function performs a minimum variance quantization. The third input parameter to the rgb2ind function – 'nodither' – specifies the behavior of the function regarding *dithering* process[3] which is not recommended for this type of application[4]. The histogram of the quantized indexed image x_q with a colormap cmap_q is obtained with the imhist function, and lines 11–12 sort the histogram in descending order to present the dominant colors of the image from left to right. The bar function is used to plot the sorted histogram, and line 14 sets the colors of the bars with the image's quantized colors themselves so that we obtain our combined color histogram of the input image.

LISTING 10.2
Color quantization and dominant colors.

```
1  % Color quantization and dominant colors
2  img = imread('flamingos.jpg');
3  % img = imread('lighthouse.png');
4  figure, imshow(img)
5
6  n = 8;
7  [img_q,cmap_q] = rgb2ind(img,n,'nodither');
8  figure, imshow(img_q,cmap_q)
9
10 hx_q = imhist(img_q,cmap_q);
11 [hx_qs,idx] = sort(hx_q,'descend');
12 cmap_qs = cmap_q(idx,:);
13 figure, b = bar(hx_qs,'FaceColor','flat');
14 b.CData = cmap_qs;
15 if n == 1
16     xticks(1), xticklabels(0)
17 else
18     xticks([1 n]), xticklabels([0 n-1])
19 end
```

Figure 10.4 shows the results for two different images (parts (a) and (d)) for eight quantized colors. The quantized images are shown in parts (b) and (e), and the respective histograms are displayed in parts (c) and (f). We can see that the pinkish flamingo colors are the fourth dominant color in the

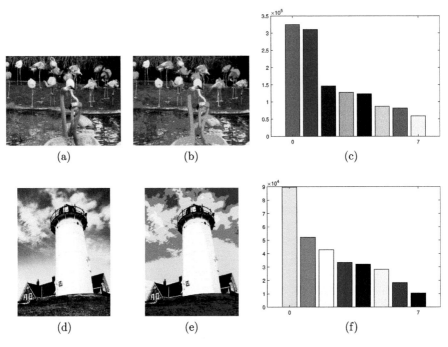

FIGURE 10.4
Reduction of the number of colors using color quantization with the rgb2ind function, and the respective combined color histograms. Original images: courtesy of The MathWorks.

top image, whereas, for the lighthouse image, the first two dominant colors correspond to the sky.

The number of quantized colors, denoted as n, is determined based on the following rationale: a histogram incorporating many colors might undermine the effectiveness of summarizing the image's color palette. Conversely, selecting too small a number could lead to a quantization process that clusters significantly distinct colors together.

An example is shown in Figure 10.5: for $n = 4$, the reddish and greenish colors of the input image (part (a)) were grouped in the quantized image (part (b)). The minimum variance quantization algorithm considers the actual distribution of colors in the image, allocating more quantized colors to those that appear more frequently in the image. In the example, two quantized colors were allocated to the bluish portion of the input image (colors 0 and 3 in the histogram in part (c)), and only one quantized color was allocated to the reddish and greenish portions of the input image (color 1 in the histogram in part (c)).

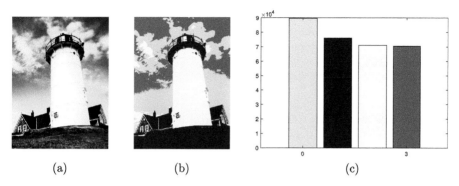

(a) (b) (c)

FIGURE 10.5
Color quantization (b) and histogram (c) of the image lighthouse.png (a), for $n = 4$. Original image: courtesy of The MathWorks.

Discussion (Recipe notes)

In this recipe, you learned how to compute and display combined color histograms and dominant colors of an image. We used the rgb2ind function to reduce the number of colors with the *minimum variance quantization* method. We encourage you to explore additional color quantization options (see links below for resources).

Learn more about it

Useful MATLAB functions

Type the function name in the search field at www.mathworks.com/help/matlab/
· bar [5.] cmunique · colorcloud · imapprox · impixelregion · rgb2ind ·

MATLAB documentation, demos, and examples

- Reduce the Number of Colors in an Image
  www.mathworks.com/help/images/reduce-the-number-of-colors-in-an-image.html

Notes

1 The recipe has been prepared using MATLAB's built-in images.
2 Rotation was performed interactively, using the mouse.

3   Dithering is a technique used in image processing to create the illusion of color depth and detail in images with a limited color palette. It involves intentionally applying noise or fine patterns to reduce the appearance of color banding or quantization errors.
4   Dithering can make the image look more detailed, but the original color information is potentially lost. If the goal is to determine the dominant colors, dithering can confuse the issue by spreading the color errors around and making it difficult to identify the primary colors in the image.
5   There are several functions with the same name in MATLAB. In this case, we are interested in the one at: `www.mathworks.com/help/matlab/ref/bar.html`.

Part IV

Point transformations

Part IV – Point transformations

The recipes in Part IV focus on *point operations* whose common goal is to **enhance** an image. The enhancement results are sometimes targeted at a human viewer (e.g., contrast adjustment or gamma correction). In contrast, in other instances, the results may be more suitable for subsequent processing stages in a machine vision system (e.g., compensating for non-uniform illumination).

Recipe 11 teaches how to implement point transformation techniques using MATLAB's built-in functions.

Recipe 12 introduces look-up tables (LUTs) and shows how they can be used to create custom point transformation functions.

Recipe 13 teaches how to perform gamma correction programmatically using MATLAB.

Recipe 14 addresses the problem of leveling non-uniform illumination and offers two methods to solve it.

DOI: 10.1201/9781003170198-14

11

Recipe 11: Intensity transformation functions

This recipe teaches you how to modify the pixel contents of monochrome images using point transformation techniques available as library functions in MATLAB.

Point operations apply the same mathematical function – often called *transformation function* – to all pixels, regardless of their location in the image or the values of their neighbors.

Transformation functions in the spatial domain can be expressed as:

$$g(x, y) = T\left[f(x, y)\right] \qquad (11.1)$$

where $g(x, y)$ is the processed image, $f(x, y)$ is the original image, and T is an operator on $f(x, y)$.

Since the actual coordinates do not play any role in the way the transformation function processes the original image, a shorthand notation can be used:

$$s = T\left[r\right] \qquad (11.2)$$

where r is the original gray level, and s is the resulting gray level after processing.

Point transformations may be *linear* (e.g., negative), *piecewise-linear* (e.g., gray level slicing), or *non-linear* (e.g., gamma correction). Figure 11.1 shows examples of basic linear (*identity* and *negative*) and non-linear (*log, inverse log, power*, and n^{th} *root*) transformation functions.

Point operations are usually treated as simple mapping operations whereby the new pixel value at a specific location depends only on the original pixel value at that same location and the mapping function. In other words, the resulting image does not exhibit any change in size, geometry, or local structure if compared with the original image.

DOI: 10.1201/9781003170198-15

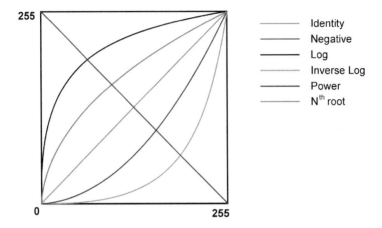

FIGURE 11.1
Basic intensity transformation functions.

You will need (Ingredients)

- MATLAB R2012b or later
- MATLAB Image Processing Toolbox (IPT)
- (OPTIONAL[1]) One or more of your images

Steps (Preparation)

This recipe focuses on point transformation techniques available as library functions in MATLAB, particularly imadjust (for contrast adjustment) and imcomplement (for computing the negative of an image). The process consists of these steps:

1. Open input image.
2. Select a MATLAB library function that performs the desired transformation.
3. Apply the transformation function to the input image.
4. (OPTIONAL) Display *before* and *after* images and other relevant plots (e.g., transformation function) and values.

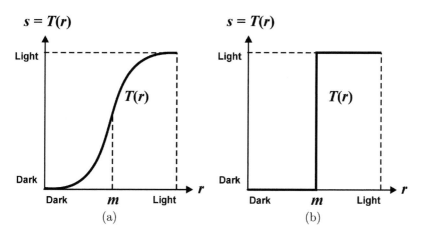

FIGURE 11.2
Examples of gray level transformations for contrast enhancement. Redrawn from [12].

Examples

Part 1: Contrast adjustment

One of the most common applications of point transformation functions is *contrast manipulation* (also known by many other names, such as *contrast stretching*, *gray level stretching*, *contrast adjustment*, and *amplitude scaling*). These functions often exhibit a curve that resembles a sigmoid function (Figure 11.2(a)): pixel values of $r < m$ are compressed towards darker values in the output image, whereas values of $r > m$ are mapped to brighter pixel values in the resulting image. The slope of the curve indicates how dramatic the contrast changes will be; in its most extreme case, a contrast manipulation function degenerates into a binary thresholding[2] function (Figure 11.2(b)), where pixels in the input image whose value is $r < m$ become black and pixels whose value is $r > m$ are converted to white.

One of the most valuable variants of contrast adjustment functions is the *automatic contrast adjustment* (or simply *auto-contrast*), a point transformation that – for images of class `uint8` in MATLAB – maps the darkest pixel value in the input image to 0, the brightest pixel value to 255, and redistributes the intermediate values linearly (Figure 11.3).

The autocontrast function can be described as:

$$s = \frac{L-1}{r_{max} - r_{min}} \cdot (r - r_{min}) \tag{11.3}$$

where: r is the pixel value in the original image (in the [0, 255] range), r_{max} and r_{min} are the values of its brightest and darkest pixels, s is the resulting

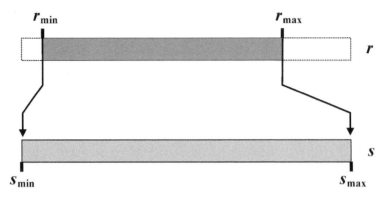

FIGURE 11.3
Auto-contrast operation. Redrawn from [10].

FIGURE 11.4
Contrast adjustment. Original image: courtesy of The MathWorks.

pixel value, and $L - 1$ is the highest gray value that can be encoded in the input image (usually $L = 256$).

Listing 11.1 shows how to apply the auto-contrast transformation function to an input image with poor contrast. It uses `imadjust` with the simplest possible syntax (i.e., default options for input and output gray level range). According to the documentation, in this case, "`imadjust` saturates the bottom 1% and the top 1% of all pixel values." The overall result is an increase in the contrast of the image. Figure 11.4 shows the images before and after processing.

FIGURE 11.5
Image adjustment with a customized range of gray levels of interest. Original image: courtesy
of The MathWorks.

LISTING 11.1
Auto-contrast.

```
% Auto-contrast
img_1 = imread('pout.tif');
img_2 = imadjust(img_1);
montage({img_1, img_2})
```

Listing 11.2 uses imadjust with *customized* options for input and output
gray level range (r_{min}, r_{max}, s_{min}, and s_{max}) selected to provide a more
dramatic contrast effect on the image. Note that these values are normalized to the [0, 1.0] range (lines 2–3) to comply with the imadjust function.
Figure 11.5 shows the images before and after processing.

LISTING 11.2
Auto-contrast with specified range.

```
% Auto-contrast with specified range
r_min = 100/255; r_max = 140/255;
s_min = 5/255; s_max = 250/255;
img_1 = imread('pout.tif');
img_2 = imadjust(img_1,[r_min r_max],[s_min s_max]);
montage({img_1, img_2})
```

Contrast adjustment can also be applied to color images but should be used
carefully since it might result in hue changes in the output image. Listing 11.3
uses imadjust with an input RGB color image. Figure 11.6 shows the images
before and after processing.

FIGURE 11.6
Image adjustment applied to a color image. Original image: courtesy of The MathWorks.

LISTING 11.3
Auto-contrast for a color image.

```
1 % Auto-contrast for color image
2 img_1 = imread('football.jpg');
3 img_2 = imadjust(img_1,[.2 .3 0; .6 .7 1],[]);
4 montage({img_1, img_2})
```

Part 2: Negative

Listing 11.4 shows how to apply the negative transformation function to an image using `imcomplement`. The negative point transformation function is used whenever it makes the output more suitable for the task at hand (e.g., by making it easier to notice interesting details in the image or making the convention of background and foreground pixels in binary images[3] consistent with subsequent steps in the pipeline). Figure 11.7 shows the images before and after processing for binary, grayscale, and color images.

LISTING 11.4
Negative transformation function.

```
1  % Negative transformation function
2
3  % Binary image
4  img_1 = imread('text.png');
5  img_2 = imcomplement(img_1);
6  montage({img_1, img_2})
7
8  % Grayscale image
9  img_1 = imread('cameraman.tif');
10 img_2 = imcomplement(img_1);
11 montage({img_1, img_2})
12
13 % Color image
14 img_1 = imread('football.jpg');
15 img_2 = imcomplement(img_1);
16 montage({img_1, img_2})
```

FIGURE 11.7
Negative of an image for binary (top), grayscale (center), and color (bottom) images. Original images: courtesy of The MathWorks.

Discussion (Recipe notes)

In this recipe, you have learned how to apply simple point transformation functions to enhance the contrast of an image, including cases where you specify the input and output ranges for the stretching operation. MATLAB has a function, stretchlim, that can assist you in finding the best upper and lower limits for contrast stretching and includes an option where you can specify the fraction of the image to saturate at low and high pixel values.

You have also learned how to compute the negative of an image using imcomplement.

You are encouraged to expand upon each example in this recipe, for example, by performing contrast adjustment interactively, using the MATLAB *Adjust Contrast* tool.

Learn more about it

Useful MATLAB functions

Type the function name in the search field at www.mathworks.com/help/matlab/
  · imadjust · imcomplement · stretchlim ·

MATLAB documentation, demos, and examples

- Adjust Contrast Tool
  www.mathworks.com/help/images/ref/imcontrast.html
- Adjust Image Intensity Values to Specified Range
  www.mathworks.com/help/images/adjust-image-intensity-values-to-specified-range.html
- Contrast Enhancement Techniques
  www.mathworks.com/help/images/contrast-enhancement-techniques.html

Notes

1 The recipe has been prepared using MATLAB's built-in images.
2 See Recipe 18.
3 See Part VII.

12

Recipe 12: Custom point transformation functions

This recipe teaches you how to implement any type of point transformation function using look-up tables (LUTs).

You will need (Ingredients)

- MATLAB R2020b or later
- MATLAB Image Processing Toolbox (IPT)
- Image file: `vpfig.png`
- (OPTIONAL[1]) One or more of your images

Steps (Preparation)

The process consists of these steps:

1. Load input image.
2. Create a point transformation function expressed as a look-up table (LUT).
3. Apply the transformation function to the input image.
4. (OPTIONAL) Display *before* and *after* images and other relevant plots (e.g., transformation function) and values.

Part 1: Linear functions

Listing 12.1 shows how to create an identity transformation function, which simply maps each pixel value to the same value. Figure 12.1 part (a) shows a plot of the transformation function whereas parts (b) and (c) display the input

DOI: 10.1201/9781003170198-16

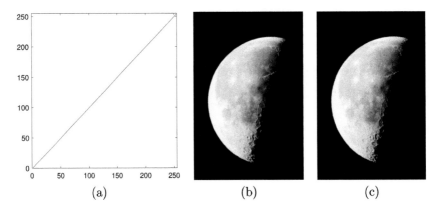

FIGURE 12.1
Identity transformation. (a) Plot of the identity transformation function. (b) Input image. (c) Output image. Original image: courtesy of The MathWorks.

and output images – which, in this case, have identical contents (which has been confirmed using `isequal` in the code).

LISTING 12.1
Identity point transformation function.

```
1  % Identity point transformation function
2  identity_function = uint8(0:255);
3  plot(identity_function); xlim([0 255]); ylim([0 255]);
4
5  img_1 = imread('moon.tif');
6  img_2 = intlut(img_1, identity_function);
7  figure, montage({img_1, img_2})
8
9  if isequal(img_1, img_2)
10     disp("The two images are identical.")
11 end
```

Listing 12.2 shows how to create the negative transformation function (also known as *contrast reverse* [21]), which generates the negative of an image. The negative point transformation function is used whenever it makes the output more suitable for the task at hand (e.g., by making it easier to notice interesting details in the image). Figure 12.2 part (a) shows a plot of the transformation function whereas part (b) displays the input and output images – which, in this case, are the negative of each other (which has been confirmed using `isequal` and the library function `imcomplement`[2] in the code).

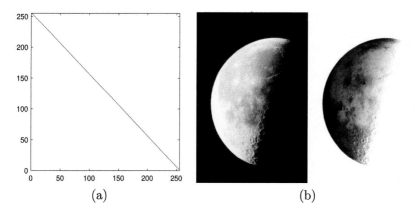

(a)   (b)

FIGURE 12.2
Negative transformation. (a) Plot of the negative transformation function. (b) Left: input image; right: output image. Original image: courtesy of The MathWorks.

LISTING 12.2
Negative point transformation function.

```
 % Negative point transformation function
 negative_function = uint8(255:-1:0);
 plot(negative_function); xlim([0 255]); ylim([0 255]);

 img_1 = imread('moon.tif');
 img_2 = intlut(img_1, negative_function);
 figure, montage({img_1, img_2})

 if isequal(img_2, imcomplement(img_1))
     disp("The two images are the negative of each other.")
 end
```

Part 2: Piecewise-linear functions

Piecewise-linear transformations can be described by two or more linear equations, one for each interval of gray level values in the input image.

Listing 12.3 shows how the piecewise-linear transformation function specified by Eq. (12.1) can be implemented using a lookup table (LUT) (and the `intlut` function) in MATLAB. Figure 12.3 part (a) shows a plot of the transformation function, whereas part (b) displays the input and output images.

$$s = \begin{cases} 2 \cdot f & \text{for } 0 < r \le 64 \\ 128 & \text{for } 64 < r \le 128 \\ f & \text{for } r > 128 \end{cases} \qquad (12.1)$$

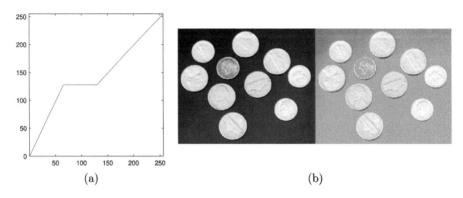

FIGURE 12.3
Piecewise-linear transformation. (a) Plot of the piecewise-linear transformation function specified by Eq. (12.1). (b) Left: input image; right: output image. Original image: courtesy of The MathWorks.

LISTING 12.3
Piecewise-linear point transformation function.

```
 1  % Piecewise-linear point transformation function
 2
 3  my_lut = uint8(zeros([1 256]));
 4  my_lut(1:65) = 2*(0:64);
 5  my_lut(66:129) = 128;
 6  my_lut(130:256) = (130:256)-1;
 7
 8  plot(my_lut), axis tight, axis square
 9
10  img_1 = imread('coins.png');
11  img_2 = intlut(img_1,my_lut);
12
13  figure, montage({img_1, img_2})
```

Part 3: Non-linear functions

There are many useful non-linear point transformation functions in image processing, including logarithmic, power law, and sigmoid functions. Essentially, if you know how to express the function mathematically, you should be able to implement it using the same recipe as before.

Listing 12.4 shows how to create logarithmic transformation functions, which can be used to compress the dynamic range of an image to bring out features that were not originally as clear.

Log transformations can be mathematically described as:

$$s = c \cdot \log(1 + r) \tag{12.2}$$

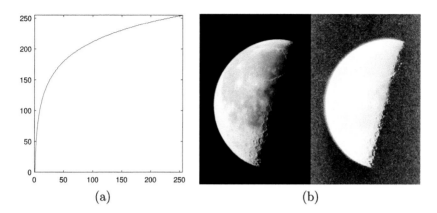

FIGURE 12.4
Logarithmic transformation. (a) Plot of the log transformation function specified by Eq. (12.2).
(b) Left: input image; right: output image. Original image: courtesy of The MathWorks.

where: r is the original pixel value, s is the resulting pixel value, and c is a
constant.

LISTING 12.4
Logarithmic transformation function.

```
% Logarithmic function

x = 0:255; c = 255 / log(256);
log_function = uint8(c * log(x + 1));
plot(log_function); xlim([0 255]); ylim([0 255]);

img_1 = imread('moon.tif');
img_2 = intlut(img_1, log_function);
figure, montage({img_1, img_2})
```

Figure 12.4 part (a) shows a plot of the transformation function, whereas
part (b) displays the input and output images.

The log transformation and its inverse are non-linear transformations
used, respectively, when we want to compress or expand the dynamic range
of pixel values in an image.

The inverse of the log function is as follows.

$$s = \exp(r/c) - 1 \tag{12.3}$$

where: r is the original pixel value, s is the resulting pixel value, and c is a
constant.

Listing 12.5 shows how to apply the *inverse* logarithmic transformation
to "undo" the changes made by the log transformation to the image and
computes the absolute difference between the initial image and the final image (after having applied the log transformation followed by the inverse

log transformation). Figure 12.5 part (a) shows a plot of the transformation function, whereas part (b) displays the input, intermediate, and output images.

LISTING 12.5
Inverse logarithmic transformation function.

```
 % Inverse log function

 x = 0:255; c = 255 / log(256);
 inverse_log_function = uint8(exp(x/c) - 1);
 plot(inverse_log_function); xlim([0 255]); ylim([0 255]);

 img_1 = imread('moon.tif');
 img_2 = intlut(img_1, log_function);
 img_3 = intlut(img_2, inverse_log_function);
 figure, montage({img_1, img_2, img_3})

 img_diff = imabsdiff(img_1, img_3);

 figure, imshow(img_diff,[])
 num_non_zero_pixels = nnz(img_diff);
 total_num_pixels = numel(img_diff);
 percent_non_zero_pixels = 100 * num_non_zero_pixels/total_num_pixels;
 brightest_pixel_value = max(img_diff(:));

 sprintf("There are %d non-zero pixels in the difference image" + ...
     " (corresponding to %.1f percent of the total image)", ...
     num_non_zero_pixels, percent_non_zero_pixels)

 sprintf("The brightest pixels value in img_diff is " + ...
     "%d (in a [0..255] range)", brightest_pixel_value)
```

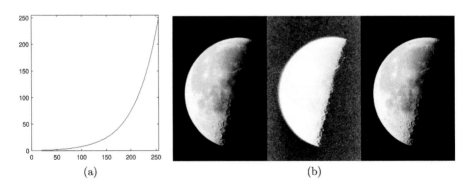

(a)   (b)

FIGURE 12.5
Logarithmic and inverse logarithmic transformations. (a) Plot of the inverse log transformation function specified by Eq. (12.3). (b) Left: input image; center: image after log transformation; right: output image obtained by applying the inverse log transformation. Original image: courtesy of The MathWorks.

FIGURE 12.6
Difference image after log transformation followed by inverse log transformation. Original image: courtesy of The MathWorks.

Note that, at first glance, the output image looks identical to the input image. This is not entirely true: a closer inspection shows minor differences in some pixel values, caused by the need to round to the nearest uint8 value when building the LUTs for both log and inverse log transformations. Figure 12.6 shows the differences, emphasized for display purposes. The code in Listing 12.5 will also produce descriptive messages indicating that "There are 39677 non-zero pixels in the difference image (corresponding to 20.6 percent of the total image)" and "The brightest pixels in the final image have a gray value of 3 (in a [0..255] range)."

For another example of a useful non-linear transformation function, let us create a sigmoid transformation described by:

$$s = \frac{1}{1 + \exp(-a(r - b))} \tag{12.4}$$

where: r is the original pixel value, s is the resulting pixel value, a is a parameter that defines the *slope* of the function, and b is a parameter that defines the *inflection point* of the function where $s = 0.5$.

The sigmoid transformation function can be used to increase the contrast of an image to bring out features that were not initially as clear or de-emphasize distracting aspects of the image.

Listing 12.6 shows how to create the sigmoid transformation function and apply it to an image to "clean up" the results of scanning a figure from a textbook. Figure 12.7 part (a) shows a plot of the transformation function, whereas part (b) displays the input and output images.

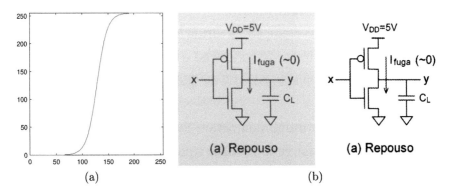

(a)   (a) Repouso   (a) Repouso
                                              (b)

FIGURE 12.7
Sigmoid transformation. (a) Plot of the sigmoid transformation function specified by Eq. (12.4).
(b) Left: input image; right: output image. Original image: courtesy of The MathWorks.

LISTING 12.6
Sigmoid transformation function.

```
% Sigmoid transformation function

x = 0:255; slope = 0.1; inflec = 127;
sigmoid_function = uint8(255./(1 + exp(-slope*(x - inflec))));
plot(sigmoid_function); xlim([0 255]); ylim([0 255]); grid on
title('Sigmoid function')

img_1 = imread('vpfig.png');
img_2 = intlut(img_1, sigmoid_function);
figure, montage({img_1, img_2})
```

To conclude this recipe, a few words about the computational efficiency gains obtained by using LUTs instead of a "naive" approach that computes the result of applying a function to each *pixel* in the input image.

Listing 12.7 shows how to implement the non-linear transformation function $s = c\sqrt{r}$, where $c = 5$ and apply it to a large image (5000×5358 pixels) using both approaches. It uses MATLAB's `tic` and `toc` functions to measure the execution time for the transformation step in each case. The results obtained by the authors[3] verify that the LUT approach is noticeably faster (in this case, by a factor of 3) than the pixel-by-pixel computation.

LISTING 12.7
Computational cost comparison: LUT versus "naive" approach.

```
% Computational cost of LUT vs. naive approach

img = imread('tumor_091R.tif');

% Direct (naive) method
img_1 = double(im2gray(img));
tic
img_2 = uint8(5 * sqrt(img_1));
```

```
 9  toc
10
11  % LUT-based method
12  my_lut = uint8(zeros([1 256]));
13  my_lut(1:256) = uint8(5 * sqrt(0:255));
14  img_3 = im2gray(img);
15
16  tic
17  img_4 = intlut(img_3, my_lut);
18  toc
```

Discussion (Recipe notes)

In this recipe, you have learned how to use lookup tables (and the `intlut` function) to create any custom point transformation function allowing you to, essentially, modify the pixel contents of an image any way you want, with direct control over the specification of the transformation function. Moreover, by implementing these functions as lookup tables (instead of naively computing the values for each pixel in the image), you have also learned how to do it in the most computationally effective way.

Learn more about it

Useful MATLAB functions

Type the function name in the search field at www.mathworks.com/help/matlab/
  · intlut · isequal · montage ·

Notes

1 The recipe has been prepared using MATLAB's built-in images and some of the authors' images, which should be available on the website for the book.
2 See Recipe 11.
3 In one of the runs, we recorded 0.27 seconds for the direct method and 0.09 seconds for the LUT-based method using a specific combination of hardware, OS, and MATLAB version. These numbers (and their ratio) may vary significantly from one setup to the next.

13

Recipe 13: Gamma correction

This recipe teaches you how to perform gamma correction on an image.

Gamma correction is a method initially devised to tackle the discrepancies between sensors and display units in analog television systems because light intensity, whether captured by the camera or reproduced on the screen, doesn't correspond linearly with voltage levels. In addition to pre-compensating for the non-linearity of the display, gamma correction has the added benefit of encoding the luminance information into a perceptually uniform space, thus compensating for the non-linear characteristics of the human visual system. Moreover, the gamma-corrected signal also becomes less sensitive to noise.

Outside of TV systems, gamma correction can be applied to individual images as a type of non-linear intensity transformation function (also known as *power-law function*), described mathematically as:

$$s = c \cdot r^{\gamma} \tag{13.1}$$

where: r is the original pixel value, s is the resulting pixel value, c is a scaling constant, and γ is a positive value. Figure 13.1 shows a plot of Equation (13.1) for several values of γ.

The `imadjust` function in MATLAB can be used to perform gamma correction with the syntax: `g = imadjust(f,[],[],gamma)`. You can limit the application of the power-law transformation to values within a range specified using the syntax:

```
J = imadjust(I,[low_in; high_in],[low_out; high_out], gamma)
```

In this case, any values below `low_in` and above `high_in` are *clipped* or simply mapped to `low_out` and `high_out`, respectively. Only values in between these limits are affected by the curve.

DOI: 10.1201/9781003170198-17

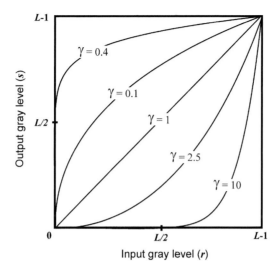

FIGURE 13.1
Examples of power-law transformations for different values of γ.

You will need (Ingredients)

- MATLAB R2012b or later
- MATLAB Image Processing Toolbox (IPT)
- (OPTIONAL[1]) One or more of your images

Steps (Preparation)

The process consists of these steps:

1. Load input image.
2. Apply the power-law transformation function to the input image using a suitable value for gamma.
3. (OPTIONAL) Display *before* and *after* images and other relevant plots (e.g., transformation function) and values.

Listing 13.1 shows how to apply gamma correction to grayscale and color images. Figures 13.2 and 13.3 show the results for three different values of gamma. Notice how the results with $\gamma = 1$ look identical to the input image (as expected), whereas those with $\gamma > 1$ and $\gamma < 1$ produce darker and brighter versions of the input image, respectively.

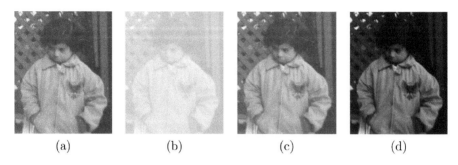

| (a) | (b) | (c) | (d) |

FIGURE 13.2
Gamma correction for grayscale images with different values of gamma. (a) Input image. (b)
Output image for $\gamma < 1$. (c) Output image for $\gamma = 1$. (d) Output image for $\gamma > 1$. Original
image: courtesy of The MathWorks.

| (a) | (b) | (c) | (d) |

FIGURE 13.3
Gamma correction for color images with different values of gamma. (a) Input image. (b) Output
image for $\gamma < 1$. (c) Output image for $\gamma = 1$. (d) Output image for $\gamma > 1$. Original image:
courtesy of The MathWorks.

LISTING 13.1
Gamma correction.

```
% Gamma correction

% Grayscale image
img_1 = imread('pout.tif');
imshow(img_1), title("Original image")
for gamma = 0.5:0.5:1.5
    img_2 = imadjust(img_1, [], [], gamma);
    figure, imshow(img_2), title(sprintf("Gamma = %.1f",gamma))
    imwrite(img_2,sprintf("result_gamma_gray_%.1f.png", gamma));
end

% Color image
img_1 = imread('football.jpg');
figure, imshow(img_1), title("Original image")
for gamma = 0.5:0.5:1.5
    img_2 = imadjust(img_1, [], [], gamma);
    figure, imshow(img_2), title(sprintf("Gamma = %.1f",gamma))
    imwrite(img_2,sprintf("result_gamma_color_%.1f.png", gamma));
end
```

Discussion (Recipe notes)

In this recipe, you learned how to perform gamma correction (a non-linear transformation function used for brightness and contrast adjustment) using the built-in MATLAB function, `imadjust` (initially introduced in Recipe 11). You might want to try implementing gamma correction "from scratch" using a LUT (see Recipe 12) and compare the results.

   You might also want to explore the `lin2rgb` function and experiment with its rich options to control the output color gamut and make it comply with standards, such as sRGB, Adobe RGB (1998), or ProPhoto (ROMM RGB).

Learn more about it

Useful MATLAB functions

Type the function name in the search field at www.mathworks.com/help/matlab/
   · `imadjust` · `intlut` · `lin2rgb` ·

Note

1   The recipe has been prepared using MATLAB's built-in images and some of the authors' images, which should be available on the website for the book.

14

Recipe 14: Leveling non-uniform illumination

This recipe teaches you how to correct for non-uniform illumination when binarizing a grayscale image.

The process of *image binarization* (described in detail in Recipe 18) using thresholding is highly sensitive to the (background) illumination of a scene. Even "easy-to-binarize" images (which usually show a bimodal histogram corresponding to concentrations of foreground and background pixels) pose a much more complex challenge if the illumination pattern changes from constant (uniform) to gradual.

In this recipe, you will learn how to successfully binarize images to compensate for non-uniform illumination using two different methods: (1) adaptive thresholding; and (2) morphological image processing operations.

You will need (Ingredients)

- MATLAB R2016a or later
- MATLAB Image Processing Toolbox (IPT)
- (OPTIONAL[1]) One or more of your images

Steps (Preparation)

Method 1: Adaptive thresholding

For background illumination correction using adaptive thresholding, the main steps are:

1. Load a grayscale image into the workspace.
2. Compute the adaptive threshold, which represents an estimate of average background illumination.

DOI: 10.1201/9781003170198-18

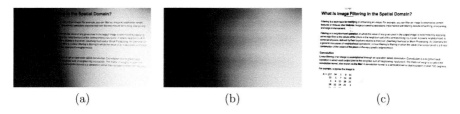

(a)   (b)   (c)

FIGURE 14.1
Background illumination correction using adaptive thresholding. Original image: courtesy of The MathWorks.

3. Binarize the grayscale image using the computed threshold.

4. (OPTIONAL) Display *before* and *after* images and other relevant plots (e.g., original image's histogram), images, and numerical values.

The code in Listing 14.1 illustrates how to perform adaptive thresholding in MATLAB. Note that the adaptthresh function takes a second parameter that represents the *sensitivity* (a scalar in the range [0 1.0]) and a third parameter 'ForegroundPolarity', used to determine which pixels are considered foreground pixels[2].

LISTING 14.1
Handling non-uniform illumination (Method 1: adaptive thresholding).

```
1 % Handling non-uniform illumination
2 % Method 1: adaptive thresholding
3
4 img_1 = imread('printedtext.png');
5 img_2 = adaptthresh(img_1,0.4,'ForegroundPolarity','dark');
6 img_3 = imbinarize(img_1,img_2);
7 figure, montage({img_1, img_2,img_3})
```

Figure 14.1 shows the original image (a), the extracted background illumination pattern (b), and the resulting binarized image (c).

Method 2: Morphological image processing

For background illumination correction using morphological operations, the main steps are:

1. Load a grayscale image into the workspace.

2. Define an appropriately shaped *structuring element* with a size commensurate with the size of the foreground objects in the image.

3. Perform morphological opening using the structuring element from the previous step to obtain an estimate of the background illumination pattern.

4. Subtract the background approximation image from the original image.

5. Adjust the contrast of the resulting image.

6. Binarize the grayscale image.

7. (OPTIONAL) Display *before* and *after* images and other relevant plots (e.g., original image's histogram), images, and numerical values.

Listing 14.2 illustrates the steps above.

LISTING 14.2
Handling non-uniform illumination (Method 2: morphological image processing).

```
1  % Handling non-uniform illumination
2  % Method 2: morphological image processing
3
4  img_1 = imread('rice.png');
5  se = strel('disk',15);
6  background = imopen(img_1,se); % estimate of background
7  img_3 = img_1 - background;
8  img_4 = imadjust(img_3);
9  img_5 = imbinarize(img_4);
10 figure, montage({img_1, background, img_3, img_5})
```

Figure 14.2 shows the original image (a), the extracted background illumination pattern (b), the result of subtracting the background from the original image (c), and the resulting binarized image (d).

Discussion (Recipe notes)

In this recipe, you learned how to compensate for non-uniform illumination when performing image binarization using two different approaches. However, as you likely observed, neither method serves as a universal solution applicable to every image.

The first method uses the built-in MATLAB function adaptthresh and provides an elegant solution independent of the actual size and shape of the foreground objects of interest. Despite its elegance, finding the best value for the *sensitivity* parameter passed to adaptthresh might require some trial and error.

The second method uses a clever combination of morphological operations and image subtraction before applying a conventional (i.e., non-adaptive) binarization function, imbinarize. In our example, the selected structuring element shape (disk) and size (radius of 15 pixels) were particularly convenient for this specific image (where the foreground objects were rice grains whose main axis is less than 30 pixels long).

(a)   (b)

(c)   (d)

FIGURE 14.2
Background illumination correction using morphological image processing. Original image: courtesy of The MathWorks.

Learn more about it

Useful MATLAB functions

Type the function name in the search field at www.mathworks.com/help/matlab/
  · adaptthresh · imadjust · imbinarize · imopen · imopen · montage ·

Notes

1   The recipe has been prepared using MATLAB's built-in images.
2   In this case, since the image consists of dark text on a bright background, we have to explicitly indicate so.

Part V

Spatial filtering and special effects

Part V – Spatial filtering and special effects

The recipes in Part V focus on *image filtering operations,* whose common goal is to modify the pixel values of an input image to enhance its appearance and make it more attractive to a human viewer.

Recipe 15 teaches how to implement smoothing filters using MATLAB.
Recipe 16 shows how to create sharpening filters.
Recipe 17 provides the algorithmic version of common artistic filters used in image manipulation and image-sharing apps.

DOI: 10.1201/9781003170198-19

15

Recipe 15: Smoothing filters

This recipe teaches you how to perform linear and non-linear filtering for image smoothing based on neighborhood-oriented operations.

Smoothing filters are designed to preserve an image's coarser details and homogeneous areas while reducing some of its fine details. Smoothing filters can be used to: (i) reduce the amount of noise in the image (see the median filter example); (ii) blur the image contents (see the mean filter example); or (iii) soften the image in a visually pleasing way (see the Gaussian blur example).

You will need (Ingredients)

- MATLAB R2015a or later
- MATLAB Image Processing Toolbox (IPT) version R2015a or later
- (OPTIONAL[1]) One or more of your images

Steps (Preparation)

The process of image smoothing in MATLAB usually follows these steps and illustrates them for four different options of filters:

1. Load input image.
2. Design convolution mask (filter, kernel) either manually or using `fspecial`.
3. Apply the filter using `imfilter`.
4. Display and/or save output image.

DOI: 10.1201/9781003170198-20

(a)   (b)

FIGURE 15.1
Smoothing an image with a uniform averaging mask of 3×3 size. (a) Original image; (b) filtered image. Original image: courtesy of The MathWorks.

Option 1: Mean filter

Listing 15.1 illustrates how to perform image smoothing using a uniform averaging 3×3 mask in MATLAB. The input and output images are shown in Figure 15.1. You might want to repeat the process for different mask sizes and compare the results – the larger the size of the mask, the greater the blurring effect.

LISTING 15.1
Mean filter.

```
1  % Mean filter
2  img_1 = imread('football.jpg'); % load image
3  h_ave = fspecial('average',3); % create mean mask of size 3 by 3
4  img_1_ave = imfilter(img_1,h_ave); % filter the image
5  figure % initialize figure
6  subplot(1,2,1), imshow(img_1), title('Original Image');
7  subplot(1,2,2), imshow(img_1_ave), title('Smoothed Image');
```

Option 2: Non-uniform averaging filter

The mean filter we just implemented is known as *box filter*, and it is a uniform filter – all mask coefficients have the same value (e.g., 1/9 for a 3×3 mask).

The non-uniform version of the mean filter gives the center of the mask (the pixel in question) a higher weighted value, while all other coefficients are weighted by their distance from the center[2]:

$$h(x,y) = \frac{1}{16} \begin{bmatrix} 1 & 2 & 1 \\ 2 & 4 & 2 \\ 1 & 2 & 1 \end{bmatrix} \tag{15.1}$$

(a)   (b)

FIGURE 15.2
Smoothing an image with a non-uniform averaging mask. (a) Original image; (b) filtered image.
Original image: courtesy of The MathWorks.

Listing 15.2 illustrates how to perform non-uniform average filtering in
MATLAB. Note that `fspecial` does not provide this type of mask, so we
must create it ourselves, following Equation 15.1. The result is shown in
Figure 15.2.

LISTING 15.2
Non-uniform averaging filter.

```
% Nonuniform averaging filter
img_1 = imread('football.jpg'); % load image
h_non = (1/16).*[1 2 1; 2 4 2; 1 2 1]; % 3 by 3 nonuniform averaging mask
img_1_non = imfilter(img_1,h_non); % filter the image
figure % initialize figure
subplot(1,2,1), imshow(img_1), title('Original Image');
subplot(1,2,2), imshow(img_1_non), title('Smoothed Image');
```

Option 3: Gaussian filter

The Gaussian blur filter is the best-known example of a distanced-based non-
uniform smoothing mask. The coefficients for this mask are specified by a 2D
Gaussian function:

$$h(x, y) = \frac{1}{2\pi\sigma^2} \exp\left[\frac{-(x^2 + y^2)}{2\sigma^2}\right] \qquad (15.2)$$

It is important to note that the value of the mask at a given position x, y is
determined by two factors:

1. The Euclidean distance between a given point and the center of the
   mask.

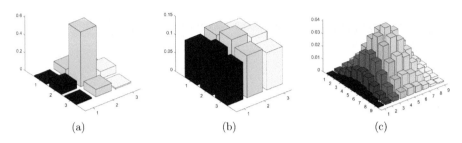

FIGURE 15.3
Gaussian masks of different sizes and σ as 3D bar plots: (a) $\sigma = 0.5$ and $s = 3$; (b) $\sigma = 2$ and $s = 3$; (c) $\sigma = 2$ and $s = 9$.

2. The value of σ, a parameter known as *standard deviation*. A larger σ will produce a more gradual (i.e., smoother) falloff from the center to the periphery.

Note that the larger the σ, the larger the size of the square mask necessary to enclose and preserve the shape of the Gaussian completely. We can use the fspecial function to try different combinations of σ and mask sizes. Listing 15.3 plots the coefficients of the filters as 3D bars (bar3 function). Results are shown in Figure 15.3. Plot (a) shows a Gaussian with $\sigma = 0.5$ into a 3×3 mask. In plot (b), one can see the effect of a Gaussian that is **not** completely enclosed in the mask – the shape of the Gaussian of $\sigma = 2$ is **not** preserved into the 3×3 mask and, in this case, the filter approximates to a box filter. Plot (c), on the other hand, shows an adequate mask size (9×9) to enclose the Gaussian of $\sigma = 2$. Note that coefficients fall off near zero at the periphery of the mask, and the shape of the Gaussian bell-shaped curve is preserved.

LISTING 15.3
Plotting Gaussian bars.

```
1  % Plot Gaussian bars
2  h_1 = fspecial('gaussian',3,0.5); % 3x3, sigma = 0.5
3  h_2 = fspecial('gaussian',3,2); % wrong: 3x3, sigma = 2
4  h_3 = fspecial('gaussian',9,2); % 9x9, sigma = 2
5  figure; % initialize figure
6  subplot(1,3,1), bar3(h_1), title('Gaussian mask h\_1');
7  subplot(1,3,2), bar3(h_2), title('Gaussian mask h\_2');
8  subplot(1,3,3), bar3(h_3), title('Gaussian mask h\_3');
```

Listing 15.4 illustrates how to perform Gaussian filtering in MATLAB using the imgaussfilt function, which requires specifying only the value of σ. In this case, the size s of the square mask is computed internally by the equation:

(a)   (b)

FIGURE 15.4
Blurring an image with a Gaussian mask of $\sigma = 0.5$ and 3×3 size. (a) Original image; (b) filtered image. Original image: courtesy of The MathWorks.

$$s = 2 \lceil 2\sigma \rceil + 1 \qquad (15.3)$$

In our example, given $\sigma = 0.5$, the size of the square mask computed using Equation 15.3 is $s = 3$, i.e., 3×3. The result is shown in Figure 15.4.

LISTING 15.4
Gaussian filter.

```
% Gaussian filter
img_1 = imread('football.jpg'); % load image
% Filter the image with a Gaussian of sigma = 0.5
img_1_gauss = imgaussfilt(img_1,0.5);
figure; % initialize figure
subplot(1,2,1), imshow(img_1), title('Original Image');
subplot(1,2,2), imshow(img_1_gauss), title('Smoothed Image');
```

After running this example, you might want to change the mask size and see what happens to the output image – the larger the size of σ, the greater the smoothing effect. You will find that changing the mask size for a Gaussian filter has a less prominent blurring effect than doing so with the averaging filter.

Option 4: Median filter

The *median filter* is the most famous example of an *order statistic filter*. This filter simply sorts all values within a window, finds the median value, and replaces the original pixel value with the median value. It is commonly used to remove *salt-and-pepper* noise from images. Because of its popularity, the median filter has its own function (`medfilt2`) in MATLAB.

(a)   (b)   (c)

FIGURE 15.5
Removing salt-and-pepper noise of a grayscale image with a median filter. (a) Original image;
(b) noisy image; (c) filtered Image. Original image: courtesy of The MathWorks.

Listing 15.5 illustrates how to perform a 3×3 median filtering on a
grayscale image degraded with salt-and-pepper noise. The result is shown
in Figure 15.5.

LISTING 15.5
Median filter applied to grayscale image.

```
% Median filter gray
img_1 = imread('pout.tif'); % load image
img_1_n = imnoise(img_1,'salt & pepper'); % add noise to image
% Filter the image with a median filter of size 3 x 3
img_1_n_med = medfilt2(img_1_n,[3 3]);
figure % initialize figure
subplot(1,3,1), imshow(img_1), title('Original Image')
subplot(1,3,2), imshow(img_1_n), title('Noisy Image')
subplot(1,3,3), imshow(img_1_n_med), title('Filtered Image')
```

You might want to repeat the process for different mask sizes and compare the results – the larger the size of the mask, the greater the smoothing
effect.

Discussion (Recipe notes)

In this recipe, you learned how to smooth an image using different techniques
– with the linear filters *mean* (also named *box filter*), *non-uniform averaging*, and
Gaussian, and with the non-linear filter *median*.

The convolution masks for the linear filters can be either created manually
by the user or using the function `fspecial`, which provides a variety of
filters for distinct applications. For example, `'laplacian'` is typically used

for image sharpening, 'log', 'prewitt', and 'sobel' for edge detection, and 'motion' to simulate the effect of camera motion on image acquisition.

The filters are applied to images using imfilter function. Among the options provided by imfilter, you can find:

- Handling image borders – Since the convolution mask is not completely inside the image matrix at the borders of the image, some of its coefficients have no corresponding image pixels to compute the multiplication. Thus, it is necessary to specify how to perform the padding of these pixels. imfilter allows for the following options.

  - Zero-padding: this is the default option. Other constant values (different from zero) can also be specified.
  - 'symmetric': image borders are mirror-reflected.
  - 'replicate': image borders are replicated.
  - 'circular': the image is considered a periodic signal; that is, it repeats in the x and y axis.

- Size of the output image:

  - 'same': this is the default option. The output image is the same size as the input image.
  - 'full': output image is larger than the input image because the values computed at the padding are also presented.

The Gaussian filter provides a "gentler" and more visually pleasant smoothing effect than the box and non-uniform averaging filters. In MATLAB, imgaussfilt function is preferred to imfilter to perform the Gaussian filtering.

The median filter, implemented by the medfilt2 function, is a non-linear filter. It can remove *outlier pixels* from an image, such as those of the salt-and-pepper noise. While imfilter and imgaussfilt accept grayscale and color images as input, as shown in our examples, medfilt2 accepts only grayscale images.

Learn more about it

Useful MATLAB functions

Type the function name in the search field at www.mathworks.com/help/matlab/

· fspecial · imfilter · imgaussfilt · imnoise · medfilt2 ·

MATLAB documentation, demos, and examples

- Filter Grayscale and Truecolor (RGB) Images using `imfilter` Function

  www.mathworks.com/help/images/filter-images-using-imfilter.html

- ROI-Based Processing

  www.mathworks.com/help/images/roi-based-processing.html

Notes

1 The recipe has been prepared using MATLAB's built-in images.
2 The further away from the center, the smaller the weight.

16

Recipe 16: Sharpening filters

This recipe teaches you how to perform image filtering to sharpen the image contents.

Sharpening filters are designed to emphasize an image's finer edges and details. This recipe presents two approaches for image sharpening: (1) unsharp masking; (2) sharpening using a Laplacian mask.

You will need (Ingredients)

- MATLAB R2013a or later
- MATLAB Image Processing Toolbox (IPT) version 2013a or later
- (OPTIONAL[1]) One or more of your images

Steps (Preparation)

1. Load input image.
2. Apply the image sharpening filter of your choice (see two options below).
3. Display and/or save output image.

Option 1: Unsharp masking

MATLAB includes the `imsharpen` function, which implements the *unsharp masking* technique. Unsharp masking consists of the following steps: (i) subtract a blurred image from its original to generate the "mask" – an image that mainly contains fine edges and details. (ii) Add the "mask" to the original image to reinforce the fine edges and details.

DOI: 10.1201/9781003170198-21

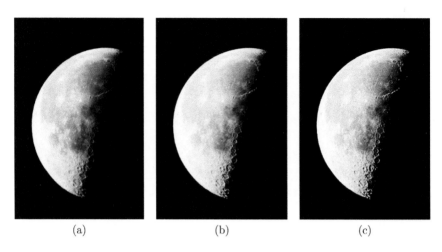

(a)   (b)   (c)

FIGURE 16.1
Sharpening using unsharp masking technique with the imsharpen function: (a) original image;
(b) 'Radius' = 1 and 'Amount' = 0.8; (c) 'Radius' = 2 and 'Amount' = 1.2. Original
image: courtesy of The MathWorks.

Listing 16.1 presents an example of image sharpening using the
imsharpen function. The 'Radius' parameter specifies the σ of the Gaussian applied internally to blur the image, whereas 'Amount' determines the
"strength" of the sharpening. The default values are 'Radius' = 1 and
'Amount' = 0.8. Results for these values are shown in Figure 16.1, part
(b). Figure 16.1, part (c) shows a more intense sharpening, obtained with
'Radius' = 2 and 'Amount' = 1.2.

LISTING 16.1
Unsharp masking.

```
1 % Unsharp Masking
2 img_1 = imread('moon.tif'); % load image
3 img_1_um1 = imsharpen(img_1); % default parameters Radius=1, Amount=0.8
4 img_1_um2 = imsharpen(img_1,'Radius',2,'Amount',1.2); % Radius=2, Amount=1
5 figure % initialize figure
6 subplot(1,3,1), imshow(img_1), title('Original Image');
7 subplot(1,3,2), imshow(img_1_um1), title('Sharpened Image 1');
8 subplot(1,3,3), imshow(img_1_um2), title('Sharpened Image 2');
```

Option 2: Sharpening using a Laplacian mask

The Laplacian is an operator that performs a second-order derivative on an
image. Although one can find variations of the Laplacian mask, the following
mask is ubiquitous:

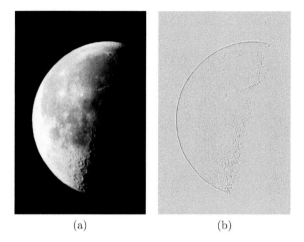

(a) (b)

FIGURE 16.2
Filtering an image with a Laplacian mask: (a) original image; (b) filtered image. Original image:
courtesy of The MathWorks.

$$h(x,y) = \begin{bmatrix} 0 & 1 & 0 \\ 1 & -4 & 1 \\ 0 & 1 & 0 \end{bmatrix} \qquad (16.1)$$

By convolving the image with the Laplacian, we can detect local intensity
transitions, mainly due to fine edges and details, as shown in Listing 16.2.
Note that we must convert the image to `double` because a Laplacian-filtered
image can result in negative values. If we were to keep the image as class
`uint8`, all negative values would be truncated and, therefore, would not accurately reflect the result of applying a Laplacian mask. By converting the
image to `double`, all negative values will remain intact. The result is shown
in Figure 16.2.

LISTING 16.2
Laplacian filter.

```
1  % Laplacian filter
2  img_1 = imread('moon.tif'); % load image
3  img_1_d = im2double(img_1); % convert to double (in the range [0...1])
4  h_lap = fspecial('laplacian',0); % create Laplacian mask
5  img_1_d_lap = imfilter(img_1_d,h_lap); % filter the image
6  figure % initialize figure
7  subplot(1,2,1), imshow(img_1), title('Original Image');
8  subplot(1,2,2), imshow(img_1_d_lap,[]), title('Laplacian output');
```

To actually *sharpen* the image, the Laplacian output and the original image have to be combined using subtraction since the central element of the
Laplacian mask in Equation 16.1 is negative. Additionally, a constant a can
be used to determine the proportion of the Laplacian output that is combined

Image processing recipes in MATLAB®

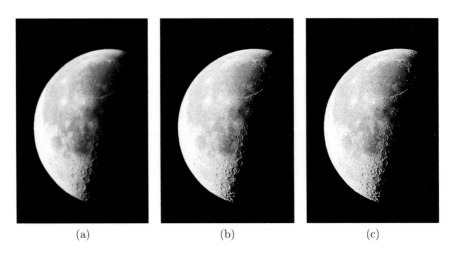

(a)   (b)   (c)

FIGURE 16.3
Sharpening using a Laplacian mask: (a) original image; (b) $a = 1.0$; (c) $a = 1.5$. Original image: courtesy of The MathWorks.

with the original image. The larger the value of a, the stronger the sharpening effect.

The code in Listing 16.3 performs image sharpening for $a = 1.0$ and $a = 1.5$. Note that we convert the sharpened images to class `uint8` before displaying, with the `im2uint8` function. Thus, pixels smaller than 0 and larger than 1 after the subtraction are truncated to 0 and 255, respectively. Figure 16.3 shows the results.

LISTING 16.3
Image sharpening using a Laplacian mask.

```
% Sharpening using a Laplacian mask
img_1 = im2double(imread('moon.tif'));
h_lap = fspecial('laplacian',0); % create Laplacian mask
img_1_lap = imfilter(img_1,h_lap); % filter the image
img_1_sha1 = img_1 - img_1_lap; % original-Laplacian, a=1.0
img_1_sha2 = img_1 - 1.5.*img_1_lap; % original-Laplacian, a=1.5
img_1_sha1 = im2uint8(img_1_sha1); % convert to uint8 (truncate)
img_1_sha2 = im2uint8(img_1_sha2); % convert to uint8 (truncate)
figure % initialize figure
subplot(1,3,1), imshow(img_1), title('Original Image');
subplot(1,3,2), imshow(img_1_sha1), title('Sharpened Image, a=1.0');
subplot(1,3,3), imshow(img_1_sha2), title('Sharpened Image, a=1.5');
```

Discussion (Recipe notes)

In this recipe, you learned how to sharpen an image using different techniques. You are encouraged to try to use the `imsharpen` function with color images and evaluate the quality of the result.

Learn more about it

Useful MATLAB functions

Type the function name in the search field at www.mathworks.com/help/matlab/
· `fspecial` · `im2uint8` · `imfilter` · `imsharpen` ·

Note

1 The recipe has been prepared using MATLAB's built-in images.

17

Recipe 17: Other image filters and special effects

This recipe teaches you how to algorithmically perform other types of image filters and special effects.

Image editors and sharing apps provide several filters designed to change the appearance of images to obtain an artistic or creative version of the original. Some of these filters do not require the user's interaction and are based on simple image processing operations. The examples in this recipe present the MATLAB implementations of the following special effects filter: (1) emboss; (2) sepia; (3) vignette; (4) posterization.

You will need (Ingredients)

- MATLAB R2016a or later
- MATLAB Image Processing Toolbox (IPT) version R2016a or later
- (OPTIONAL[1]) One or more of your images

Steps (Preparation)

1. Load input image.
2. Apply the special effect algorithm of your choice (see four options below) with the desired parameterization.
3. Display and/or save output image.

1: Emboss

The *emboss* effect is obtained using a convolution mask designed to reinforce the delicate edges of the image, following the same principle that we used to

DOI: 10.1201/9781003170198-22

(a) (b)

FIGURE 17.1
Emboss special effect. (a) Original image; (b) after embossing. Original image: courtesy of The MathWorks.

sharpen an image in Recipe 16, i.e., detecting local intensity transitions. An example of a convolution mask that provides a visible emboss effect is shown in Equation 17.1.

$$h(x,y) = \begin{bmatrix} -2 & -1 & 0 \\ -1 & 1 & 1 \\ 0 & 1 & 2 \end{bmatrix} \tag{17.1}$$

In Listing 17.1, we create the mask and use the `imfilter` function to apply it to the input image. Figure 17.1 shows the result.

LISTING 17.1
Emboss effect.

```
% Emboss
img_1 = imread('lighthouse.png'); % load image
h_emb = [-2 -1 0; -1 1 1; 0 1 2]; % create emboss mask
img_1_emb = imfilter(img_1,h_emb);% filter the image
figure % initialize figure
subplot(1,2,1), imshow(img_1), title('Original image')
subplot(1,2,2), imshow(img_1_emb), title('Emboss')
```

2: Sepia

The *sepia* is a well-known effect that gives an image the appearance of an "old photo" changing the original colors to brownish/yellowish tones. It can be implemented using a transformation matrix that linearly changes the values of the R, G, and B color channels of the pixels into new R_s, G_s, and B_s (Equation 17.2).

(a) (b)

FIGURE 17.2
Sepia special effect. (a) Original image; (b) after sepia. Original image: courtesy of The Math-Works.

$$
\begin{bmatrix} R_s \\ G_s \\ B_s \end{bmatrix} = \begin{bmatrix} 0.393 & 0.769 & 0.189 \\ 0.349 & 0.686 & 0.168 \\ 0.272 & 0.534 & 0.131 \end{bmatrix} \begin{bmatrix} R \\ G \\ B \end{bmatrix} \tag{17.2}
$$

Listing 17.2 shows how to decompose an image's color channels using `im-split`, apply the transformation matrix to each channel, and recompose the image using the `cat` function. Note that the multiplications are performed on `double`, and the results are converted back to `uint8` integers. Figure 17.2 shows the result.

LISTING 17.2
Sepia effect.

```
% Sepia
img_1 = imread('lighthouse.png');
[img_1_r,img_1_g,img_1_b] = imsplit(im2double(img_1));
img_1_r_sep = im2uint8(0.393*img_1_r + 0.769*img_1_g + 0.189*img_1_b);
img_1_g_sep = im2uint8(0.349*img_1_r + 0.686*img_1_g + 0.168*img_1_b);
img_1_b_sep = im2uint8(0.272*img_1_r + 0.534*img_1_g + 0.131*img_1_b);
img_1_sep = cat(3, img_1_r_sep, img_1_g_sep, img_1_b_sep);
figure
subplot(1,2,1), imshow(img_1), title('Original image')
subplot(1,2,2), imshow(img_1_sep), title('Sepia')
```

3: Vignette

The idea behind the *vignette* effect is to "hide" some scene elements and show only the desired ones to draw the viewer's attention. In Listing 17.3, we exemplify the concept of a vignette effect by multiplying the input by another

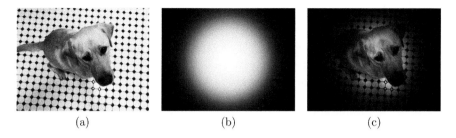

FIGURE 17.3
Vignette special effect. (a) Original image; (b) Gaussian function of $\sigma = 350$; (c) after vignette.
Original image: courtesy of The MathWorks.

image of the same dimensions containing a Gaussian function. In this implementation, the central region of the original image, corresponding to the highest values of the Gaussian, is preserved. As the Gaussian falloff nears zero, the corresponding pixels in the image fade to black. The standard deviation σ of the Gaussian (sigma variable) specifies the diameter of the vignette effect. Note that the multiplications are performed on double, and the results are converted back to uint8 integers. The mat2gray function rescales the Gaussian into the range [0, 1.0]. Figure 17.3, part (b) shows the applied Gaussian function, and part (c) shows the multiplication result.

LISTING 17.3
Vignette effect.

```
1 % Vignette
2 img_1 = im2double(imread('kobi.png'));
3 [r, c] = size(img_1,1,2);
4 sigma = 350; % standard deviation of the Gaussian
5 img_g = mat2gray(fspecial('gaussian',[r c],sigma));
6 img_1_vig = im2uint8(img_1.*img_g);
7 figure
8 subplot(1,3,1), imshow(img_1), title('Original image')
9 subplot(1,3,2), imshow(img_g), title('Gaussian')
10 subplot(1,3,3), imshow(img_1_vig), title('Vignette')
```

4: Posterization

The technique known as *posterization* was initially employed as a pre-printing process for color photographs, with the objective of minimizing the required ink colors by reducing the overall number of colors in the image [4]. In Recipe 10, we saw that the number of colors of an image could be reduced using *color quantization*, with the function rgb2ind. This recipe uses rgb2ind as part of the posterization process.

In Listing 17.4, besides reducing the number of colors to $n = 8$, we apply a median filter on the quantized image and a boundary demarcation between the different colors to perform a customized "artistic posterization." The median filter increases the homogeneity of the regions with the same color, reducing or even eliminating sparse pixels of different colors at the boundaries between them, where the tones in the original image change subtly. In this example, a median of mask size $s = 7$ is applied at each color channel of the quantized image. The detection of the boundaries between the different colors is obtained with the function `boundarymask` applied to an arbitrary color channel of the image. The output of `boundarymask` is a binary image (class `logical`), where the pixels labeled as logical "true" correspond to the boundaries. This image is an input parameter for the `imoverlay` function, which "stamps" the boundaries on the desired image. Figure 17.4 shows the results of the intermediary steps and the final artistic posterization.

LISTING 17.4
Posterization effect.

```matlab
% Posterization
img_1 = imread('lighthouse.png');

n = 8; % number of colors
[X_q,cmap_q] = rgb2ind(img_1,n,'nodither');
img_1_q = ind2rgb(X_q,cmap_q);


s = 7; % size of the median filter
img_1_q_m(:,:,1) = medfilt2(img_1_q(:,:,1),[s s]);
img_1_q_m(:,:,2) = medfilt2(img_1_q(:,:,2),[s s]);
img_1_q_m(:,:,3) = medfilt2(img_1_q(:,:,3),[s s]);

bw = boundarymask(img_1_q_m(:,:,1));
img_1_q_m_artpos = imoverlay(img_1_q_m,bw,'black');

figure
subplot(1,4,1), imshow(img_1), title('Original image')
subplot(1,4,2), imshow(img_1_q), title('Color quantized image')
subplot(1,4,3), imshow(img_1_q_m), title('Median')
subplot(1,4,4), imshow(img_1_q_m_artpos), title('Artistic posterization')
```

Discussion (Recipe notes)

In this recipe, you learned how to implement different image filters to add special effects to images. Note that we did not employ specific functions to create these special effects – they were based mainly on classic image processing techniques and MATLAB functions that we saw in former recipes.

It is worth mentioning that special effects filters are, by design, dependent on the programmer's creativity and, naturally, oriented to experimentation. You are encouraged to try your own variations of the filters presented in this recipe and design entirely new special effects filters yourself!

FIGURE 17.4

Posterization special effect, with customized operations, for an artistic result. (a) Original image; (b) quantized image with $n = 8$ colors; (c) after median filter of mask size $s = 7$. (d) artistic posterization. Original image: courtesy of The MathWorks.

Learn more about it

Useful MATLAB functions

Type the function name in the search field at www.mathworks.com/help/matlab/

· im2uint8 · im2double · imfilter · imoverlay · ind2rgb ·mat2gray·medfilt2·rgb2ind·

Note

1   The recipe has been prepared using MATLAB's built-in images.

Part VI

Image segmentation

Part VI – Image segmentation

Image segmentation is the process of partitioning an image into a set of non-overlapping regions whose union is the entire image. These regions should ideally correspond to objects and their meaningful parts, and background. Image segmentation plays a vital role in computer vision and image analysis, enabling a wide range of applications, such as object detection, tracking, recognition, and classification. Image segmentation is a challenging task, as it requires identifying the boundaries of the objects in the image and separating them from the background or other objects. Therefore, many image segmentation techniques have been developed over the years, each with its own strengths and weaknesses.

Image segmentation techniques can vary widely according to the type of image (e.g., binary, gray, color), choice of mathematical framework (e.g., morphology, image statistics, graph theory), type of features (e.g., intensity, color, texture, motion), and approach (e.g., top-down, bottom-up, graph-based).

The recipes in Part VI cover some of the most popular and useful segmentation strategies.

Recipe 18 shows how to binarize a grayscale image using *thresholding* techniques, thereby segmenting foreground objects from the (brighter or darker) background.

DOI: 10.1201/9781003170198-23

Recipe 19 shows how to use a region-based segmentation algorithm (*active contour*) to produce high-quality segmentation results.

Recipe 20 teaches how to segment an image by grouping similar pixels using the *k-means clustering* algorithm.

Recipe 21 illustrates the use of superpixel oversegmentation strategies using the simple linear iterative clustering (SLIC) algorithm.

Recipe 22 introduces the *lazy snapping* algorithm, one of the most popular graph-based segmentation methods in the literature.

18

Recipe 18: Image binarization

This recipe teaches you how to binarize a grayscale image using thresholding techniques.

The fundamental problem of thresholding is the conversion of an image with several gray levels into another image with only two gray levels (a *binary image*), usually corresponding to the notion of *foreground* (objects of interest) and a (lighter or darker) *background*. This operation is also called *binarization* in the literature. In its simplest variant (known as *global* thresholding), this conversion is performed by comparing each pixel intensity against a reference value (*threshold*, hence the name) and replacing the original pixel value with a new value that means 'white' or 'black' depending on the outcome of the comparison[1]. The most popular approach under this category was proposed by Otsu in 1979 [19] and implemented as the `graythresh` function in MATLAB. Otsu's method chooses a threshold that minimizes the intraclass variance of the thresholded black and white pixels.

Thresholding an image is a common preprocessing step in machine vision tasks in which there are relatively few objects of interest whose shape (silhouette) is more important than surface properties (such as texture) and whose average brightness is somewhat higher or lower than the other elements in the image. Hence, it can be seen as a simple segmentation technique that segments the foreground objects from the background. Once an image has been binarized, it can be processed using techniques like the ones described in Part VII of this book.

Global thresholding works well for images whose gray-level distribution (histogram) has two distinct modes, such as the one in Figure 18.1, where the narrowest and most prominent mode (on the left) corresponds to background pixels, whereas the broadest mode (on the right) reflects the intensity distribution of pixels corresponding to the coins. For more complex cases, such as the one in Figure 18.2, a more sophisticated technique, called *adaptive thresholding* is used[2].

FIGURE 18.1
A grayscale image (*coins*) (a) and its histogram (b). Original image: courtesy of The MathWorks.

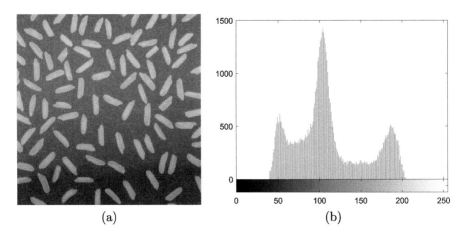

FIGURE 18.2
A grayscale image (*rice*) (a) and its histogram (b). Original image: courtesy of The MathWorks.

You will need (Ingredients)

- MATLAB R2016a or later
- MATLAB Image Processing Toolbox (IPT)
- (OPTIONAL[3]) One or more of your images

Steps (Preparation)

For binarization using a global image threshold, the main steps are:

1. Load grayscale image into the workspace.
2. Compute the threshold.
3. Binarize the grayscale image using the computed threshold.
4. (OPTIONAL) Display *before* and *after* images and other relevant plots (e.g., original image's histogram) and values (e.g., the optimal threshold computed by the *graythresh* function).

Listing 18.1 illustrates how to perform global thresholding in MATLAB. Note that `graythresh` computes the optimal threshold value based on the image's histogram, whereas `imbinarize` uses that value as a parameter to perform the binarization. In this case, the optimal threshold value is $T = 0.4941$, and the resulting image is shown in Figure 18.3.

LISTING 18.1
Global thresholding.

```
% Global thresholding
img_1 = imread('coins.png');
level = graythresh(img_1);
img_2 = imbinarize(img_1,level);
montage({img_1,img_2})
```

The steps for binarization using adaptive thresholding are essentially the same, except that now you will use the `adaptthresh` function.

Listing 18.2 illustrates how to perform adaptive thresholding in MATLAB. Note that the `adaptthresh` function takes a second parameter that represents the *sensitivity* (a scalar in the range [0, 1.0]): lower values will result in more pixels being labeled as background. Figure 18.4 shows results for three different sensitivity values.

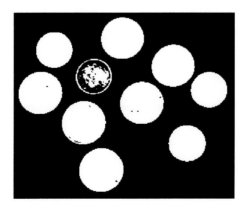

FIGURE 18.3
Binarized version of the grayscale image in Figure 18.1(a). Original image: courtesy of The Math-Works.

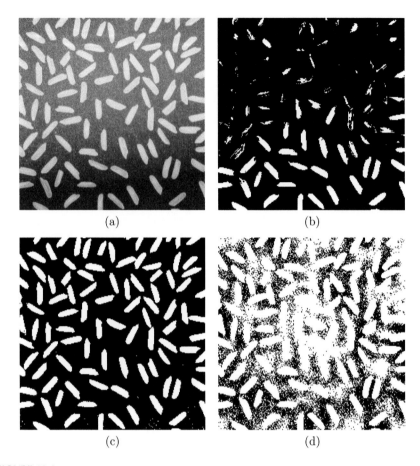

(a)   (b)

(c)   (d)

FIGURE 18.4
A grayscale image (a) and the results of image binarization using different values of sensitivity: 0.1 (b), 0.4 (c), and 0.8 (d). Original image: courtesy of The MathWorks.

LISTING 18.2
Adaptive thresholding.

```
% Adaptive thresholding

img_1 = imread('rice.png');
sensitivity = 0.4;
img_2 = adaptthresh(img_1, sensitivity);
img_3 = imbinarize(img_1,img_2);
imshowpair(img_1, img_3, 'montage')
```

Lastly, it is worth mentioning that MATLAB also includes a function called otsuthresh that computes a global threshold T *from histogram counts,* using Otsu's method [19]. When called using the syntax [T,EM] = otsuthresh(counts), the function returns the computed threshold T as well as an effectiveness metric EM, a numeric scalar in the range [0, 1.0], which indicates the effectiveness of the thresholding (an effectiveness of 1 is ideal). See Listing 18.3. For the coins image (whose histogram appears in Figure 18.1(b)), the value of EM is 0.9168 whereas for the rice image (whose histogram appears in Figure 18.2(b)), the value of EM is 0.7356.

LISTING 18.3
Otsu thresholding.

```
1  % Otsu thresholding
2
3  img_1 = imread('rice.png');
4  [counts, gray_level] = imhist(img_1,16);
5  stem(gray_level,counts)
6  [T, EM] = otsuthresh(counts);
7  img_2 = imbinarize(img_1,T);
8  figure, imshow(img_2)
```

Discussion (Recipe notes)

In this recipe, you learned how to binarize an image using built-in MATLAB functions adaptthresh, graythresh, imbinarize, otsuthresh.

You certainly have noticed that, despite their usefulness and straightforward syntax, none of the thresholding techniques are guaranteed to work "automatically" for any input image. There often is a fair amount of trial-and-error involved in getting some parameters right (such as the best value for the *sensitivity* for adaptthresh, for example). Moreover, all results are dependent on the specific image (and its grayscale distribution, i.e., histogram), and sometimes a manually chosen threshold (for global thresholding) might work better than the one computed by graythresh (see Figure 18.5)[4].

Last but certainly not least, we have seen that illumination and reflectance patterns play a critical role in thresholding. Even an easy input image (such as the coins image), which could be successfully segmented using global thresholding, poses a much harder challenge if the illumination pattern changes from constant (uniform) to gradual (Figure 18.6). The resulting image (Figure 18.7(a)) is significantly darker overall, and the corresponding histogram (Figure 18.7(b)) shows an expected shift to the left. Consequently, using the same value of threshold that produced very good results before (Figure 18.5(b)) will lead to an unacceptable binarized image (Figure 18.7(c)).

Noise can also have a significant impact on thresholding, as illustrated in Figure 18.7(d)–(f). In this case, a Gaussian noise of mean zero and variance 0.03 has been applied to the image, resulting in the image on Figure 18.7(d), whose histogram, shown in Figure 18.7(e), has lost its original bimodal shape. The result of segmenting the image using $T = 0.25$ is shown in Figure 18.7(f). Although not as bad as one could expect, it would need post-processing (noise reduction) to be truly useful.

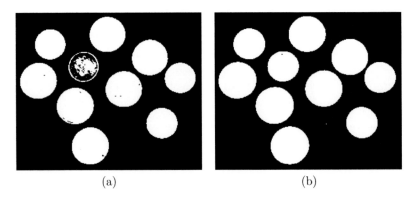

(a)   (b)

FIGURE 18.5
Image thresholding results for the *coins* image: threshold computed by Otsu's method ($T =$ 0.4941) (a) versus a manually selected threshold ($T = 0.25$) (b). Original image: courtesy of The MathWorks.

FIGURE 18.6
An example of uneven illumination pattern used to generate the image in Figure 18.7(a). Original image: courtesy of The MathWorks.

In summary, the images changed significantly in both cases, their histograms lost their bimodal shape, and the initially chosen value for the global threshold ($T = 0.25$) was no longer adequate. Additionally, no other value could be easily chosen just by inspecting the histogram and following the trial-and-error procedure suggested earlier.

Solutions to leveling non-uniform illumination and denoising the image (before binarization) are discussed in Recipes 14 and 15, respectively.

Learn more about it

Useful MATLAB functions

Type the function name in the search field at www.mathworks.com/help/ matlab/

· adaptthresh · graythresh · imbinarize · otsuthresh ·

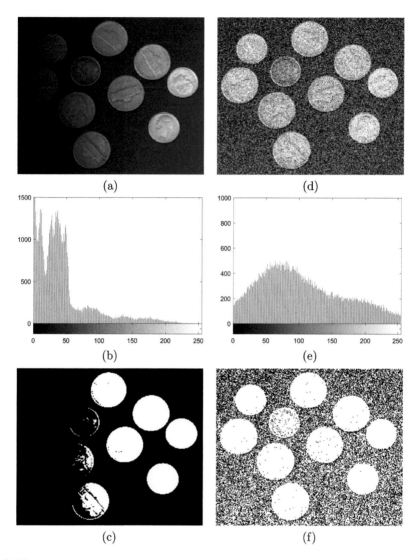

FIGURE 18.7
Effect of illumination (left) and noise (right) on thresholding. Original image: courtesy of The MathWorks.

MATLAB documentation, demos, and examples

- Getting Started with Image Segmenter
  https://www.mathworks.com/help/images/image-segmentation-using-the-image-segmenter-app.html

- Segment Image Using Thresholding in Image Segmenter
  `https://www.mathworks.com/help/images/Segment-an-Image-Using-Thresholding.html`

Notes

1   Note that the convention for 'white' or 'black' pixels being represented as 1 or 0 is *not* universal.

2   For the *rice* image, an uneven illumination pattern made an otherwise easy-to-binarize image (bright rice grains against a darker background) become harder to threshold; notice the three modes in its associated histogram. See Recipe 14 for a solution to this problem.

3   The recipe has been prepared using MATLAB's built-in images.

4   In MATLAB's *Image Segmenter* App (see references in the *Learn more about it* section), under the *Threshold* menu, you can find a friendly resource for interactive image thresholding.

19

Recipe 19: Region-based segmentation

This recipe teaches you how to perform region-based image segmentation using the active contours technique.

Region-based image segmentation algorithms are used to partition an image into regions based on similarities such as color, texture, and intensity. One approach to region-based segmentation is *active contours*, also known as *snakes*[1], which are flexible curves that can adapt to the boundaries of objects in an image. The active contour algorithm iteratively adjusts the position of the snake until it conforms to the boundaries of the object to be segmented.

In MATLAB, this is implemented by the `activecontour` function, which segments an image into the foreground (object) and background regions using a *mask* – a binary image that specifies the initial state of the active contour. The mask can be specified programmatically or interactively.

You will need (Ingredients)

- MATLAB R2013a or later
- MATLAB Image Processing Toolbox (IPT) version R2013a or later
- Image file: `bean_coffee_08.png`

Steps (Preparation)

1. Load the image into the workspace.
2. Specify an initial contour surrounding the objects of interest to serve as a mask, i.e., the region of interest (ROI).
3. Perform the segmentation operation, specifying the original image, the ROI, and the number of iterations.
4. Display *before* and *after* images and (visually) evaluate the quality of the results.

DOI: 10.1201/9781003170198-25

Listing 19.1 illustrates how to perform segmentation for three different images of different types and degrees of complexity. The first image (coins.png) is a relatively easy-to-segment grayscale image[2]. The second image (rice.png) is significantly harder to segment due to the uneven lighting pattern[3]. Lastly, the coffee beans image is a reasonably easy image to segment, which has been included in this recipe to remind you that the activecontour function can also be used for color images. The results appear in Figure 19.1.

Note that the code in Listing 19.1 uses active contours in "unsupervised mode," i.e., programmatically specifying an ROI that covers most of the image (lines 6–7, 18–19, and 30–32). The activecontour function also supports region-growing segmentation in a supervised way, i.e., interactively drawing rectangular masks surrounding the regions of interest or specifying points of interest using the mouse, to assist the segmentation algorithm[4].

The simplicity and straightforwardness of the code in Listing 19.1 hide two potentially tricky aspects that have an impact on the quality of the results:

1. The size of the ROI matters. Our code uses the entire image minus a few pixels at the border as a mask. Changing the values used to specify the border (lines 7, 19, and 32) might significantly impact the final result.

2. Getting the (maximum) number of iterations right is a trial-and-error process. The default value is 100, which leads to *very poor* results for any of these images. You might want to change the code in lines 11, 23, and 36 and see it yourself!

FIGURE 19.1
Examples of segmentation with activecontour for three test images.

LISTING 19.1

Segmentation using active contours.

```
 1  % Active contours
 2
 3  %% Image 1: coins
 4  img_1 = imread('coins.png');
 5  % Specify initial contour surrounding the objects of interest
 6  mask_1 = zeros(size(img_1));
 7  mask_1(25:end-25,25:end-25) = 1;
 8  % Display the contour
 9  figure, imshow(mask_1)
10  % Segment the image by using the activecontour function (<= 300 iterations)
11  img_1_bw = activecontour(img_1, mask_1, 300);
12  figure, imshow(img_1_bw)
13  figure, montage({img_1,img_1_bw})
14
15  %% Image 2: rice
16  img_2 = imread('rice.png');
17  % Specify initial contour surrounding the objects of interest
18  mask_2 = zeros(size(img_2));
19  mask_2(15:end-15,15:end-15) = 1;
20  % Display the contour
21  figure, imshow(mask_2)
22  % Segment the image by using the activecontour function (<= 900 iterations)
23  img_2_bw = activecontour(img_2, mask_2, 900);
24  figure, imshow(img_2_bw)
25  figure, montage({img_2,img_2_bw})
26
27  %% Image 3: coffee beans
28  img_3 = imread('bean_coffee_08.png');
29  % Specify initial contour surrounding the objects of interest
30  sz_img_3 = size(img_3);
31  mask_3 = zeros(sz_img_3(1),sz_img_3(2));
32  mask_3(45:end-45,45:end-45) = 1;
33  % Display the contour
34  figure, imshow(mask_3)
35  % Segment the image by using the activecontour function (<= 700 iterations)
36  img_3_bw = activecontour(img_3, mask_3, 700);
37  figure, imshow(img_3_bw)
38  figure, montage({img_3,img_3_bw})
```

Discussion (Recipe notes)

In this recipe, you learned how to use the activecontour function to per-form region-based segmentation on 2D grayscale and color images. This method can also be used for 3D images. Moreover, it has been integrated with the *Image Segmenter* App. See references in the *Learn more about it* section.

Beware that the active contours algorithm has many limitations, e.g., it pro-duces unacceptable results for images with complex backgrounds. Recipe 22 will show how to use graph-based algorithms for such cases.

Learn more about it

Useful MATLAB functions

Type the function name in the search field at www.mathworks.com/help/matlab/
· activecontour ·

MATLAB documentation, demos, and examples

- Getting Started with Image Segmenter App
  www.mathworks.com/help/images/image-segmentation-using-the-image-segmenter-app.html
- Image Segmentation and Analysis
  www.mathworks.com/help/images/image-analysis.html
- Segment Image Using Active Contours in Image Segmenter
  www.mathworks.com/help/images/use-active-contours-to-refine-the-segmentation.html

Notes

1   *Active contours* is the term that designates the technique in general. There are several models of active contours [23]. Depending on the context, you can find the term *snakes* referring to that specific model of *active contours*, introduced by [15].
2   See Recipe 18 for attempts to segment this image using thresholding techniques and additional insights.
3   See Recipes 14 and 18 for related discussions.
4   See links to the official documentation at the end of the recipe, for examples.

20

Recipe 20: Image segmentation using k-means clustering

This recipe teaches you how to perform image segmentation using the k-means clustering algorithm.

The main rationale behind the use of the clustering in the context of image segmentation is to *group* similar pixels into clusters, provided that – in addition to satisfying a criterion for similarity – the pixels in question are also adjacent, i.e., together they comprise a connected region of relatively uniform color. In MATLAB, the imsegkmeans function can be used to quantize gray levels or colors using k-means clustering without regard for the pixel locations[1]. Additional preprocessing can be incorporated, depending on the characteristics of the input image, to use imsegkmeans to implement more effective segmentation[2].

You will need (Ingredients)

- MATLAB R2018b or later
- MATLAB Image Processing Toolbox (IPT) version R2018b or later
- Image file: rug.png

Steps (Preparation)

For image quantization using k-means clustering, the main steps are:

1. Load an image into the workspace.
2. Select the value of K that best represents the number of distinct color regions in the image.
3. Perform k-means clustering using MATLAB's imsegkmeans function.

DOI: 10.1201/9781003170198-26

4. (OPTIONAL) Convert the result into an RGB image for easier visualization.

5. Display *before* and *after* images and (visually) evaluate the quality of the results.

Part 1: Image quantization

Listing 20.1 illustrates how to perform quantization using k-means clustering in MATLAB for different values of K, varying from 2 to 6. Note that the choice of K is crucial to determine the quality (and interpret the meaning!) of the results.

LISTING 20.1
Image segmentation using k-means clustering.

```
% Image segmentation using k-means clustering

img_1 = imread('coloredChips.png');
imshow(img_1), title("Original image")
for n_colors = 2:6
    pixel_labels = imsegkmeans(img_1,n_colors);
    pixel_labels_rgb = label2rgb(pixel_labels,'hsv');
    figure, imshow(pixel_labels,[]),title(sprintf("%d colors",n_colors))
    imwrite(pixel_labels_rgb,sprintf("result_%d_colors.png", n_colors));
end
```

Figure 20.1 shows the original image (a) and the segmentation results for $K = 2$ (b), $K = 3$ (c), $K = 4$ (d), $K = 5$ (e), and $K = 6$ (f). From a human vision perspective, the image contains five distinct foreground colors (red/orange, blue, green, and yellow chips, plus the black marker) and a relatively distinct and uncomplicated background. This means a choice of $K = 6$ should be appropriate. Inspecting the results, though, we can see that:

- The "cleanest" result was obtained for $K = 3$ (Figure 20.1 part (c)), which assumed that yellow chips belong to the background and conflated the green and blue chips and the black marker into the same cluster.

- All results for $K > 3$ (bottom row of Figure 20.1) show that the uneven illumination (the right half of the image is brighter than the left half) played a role and "forced" the algorithm to treat the background as two distinct regions[3].

- The result for part (f) ($K = 6$) is mostly correct, but – due to the algorithm's decision to split the background into two color clusters – the black marker is segmented as if it has the same colors as the green chips[4].

An elegant solution to the impact of the uneven illumination consists of converting the RGB image into another color space that separates the luminance from chrominance information, e.g., L*a*b*, and applying the `imsegkmeans` function to the color components only.

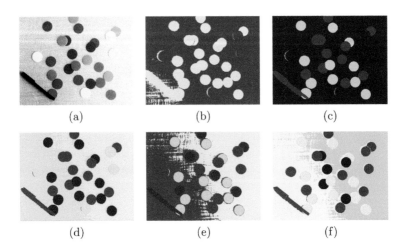

(a)   (b)   (c)

(d)   (e)   (f)

FIGURE 20.1
Image segmentation using k-means clustering, for different values of K. (a) Original image;
(b) $K = 2$; (c) $K = 3$; (d) $K = 4$; (e) $K = 5$; (f) $K = 6$. Original image: courtesy of The
MathWorks.

Listing 20.2 shows how to perform quantization using k-means clustering
on a color image converted to the L*a*b* color space for different values of K,
varying from 2 to 6. Figure 20.2 shows the original image (a) and the segmentation results for $K = 2$ (b), $K = 3$ (c), $K = 4$ (d), $K = 5$ (e), and $K = 6$ (f).
The results are in general much "cleaner" than the ones in Figure 20.1, but are
far from perfect. You might find it surprising that, for most cases, the black
marker "blends in" with the background. However, thanks to the separation
between luminance and chrominance, the uneven illumination problem only
affects the results for $K = 6$.

LISTING 20.2
Image segmentation using k-means clustering and the L*a*b* color model.

```
% Image segmentation using k-means clustering and the L*a*b* color model

img_1 = imread('coloredChips.png');
imshow(img_1), title("Original image")
img_1_lab = rgb2lab(img_1);
ab = img_1_lab(:,:,2:3); % a* and b* color components
ab = im2single(ab); % imsegkmeans requires floating point in single precis.
for n_colors = 2:6
    pixel_labels = imsegkmeans(ab, n_colors);
    pixel_labels_rgb = label2rgb(pixel_labels,'hsv');
    figure, imshow(pixel_labels,[]), title(sprintf("%d colors",n_colors))
    imwrite(pixel_labels_rgb,sprintf("result_%d_colors_lab.png", n_colors));
end
```

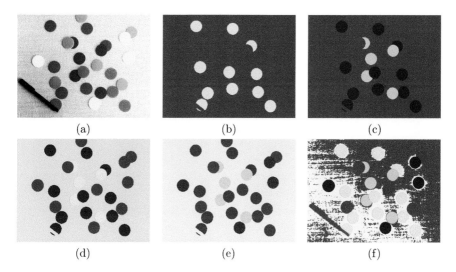

FIGURE 20.2

Image segmentation using k-means clustering in the L*a*b* color space for different values of K. (a) Original image; (b) $K = 2$; (c) $K = 3$; (d) $K = 4$; (e) $K = 5$; (f) $K = 6$. Original image: courtesy of The MathWorks.

Part 2: Image segmentation

In some cases, it is necessary to do additional processing to encode the spatial information of the image before applying the imsegkmeans function.

The code in Listing 20.3 illustrates the problem. It shows a naive attempt to segment the foreground object (in this case, a cardboard box) from the complex background (rug with similar colors) using the imsegkmeans function. As you can see (Figure 20.3), the results are *not* what you would want: the dark/bright spots on the floor are clustered together with the darker/lighter pixels belonging to the box, without any regard for the spatial location of the pixels.

LISTING 20.3

Segmentation of a more complex image using k-means clustering: first attempt.

```
% Image segmentation using k-means clustering
% First attempt
img_1 = imread('rug.png');
% Attempt to segment the image into two regions -- foreground (box)
% and background -- using k-means clustering.
labels = imsegkmeans(img_1,2);
labeled_image = labeloverlay(img_1,labels);
montage({img_1, labeled_image})
```

(a)

(b)

FIGURE 20.3
Failed attempt at image segmentation using k-means clustering and default options: (a) original image; (b) output image.

LISTING 20.4
Segmentation of a more complex image using k-means clustering: second attempt.

```
 1  % Image segmentation using k-means clustering with
 2  % texture and spatial information
 3  img_1 = imread('rug.png');
 4  % Resize the image
 5  img_1 = imresize(img_1,0.5);
 6  % Convert the image to grayscale.
 7  img_1_gray = im2gray(im2single(img_1));
 8
 9  %--------------------------
10  % Supplement the image with information about the texture in the
11  % neighborhood of each pixel. To obtain the texture information, filter a
12  % grayscale version of the image with a set of 24 Gabor filters, covering
13  % 6 wavelengths and 4 orientations.
14  wavelength = 2.^(0:5) * 3;
15  orientation = 0:45:135;
16  g = gabor(wavelength,orientation);
17  % Filter the grayscale image using the Gabor filters.
18  gabor_mag = imgaborfilt(img_1_gray,g);
19  % Smooth each filtered image to remove local variations.
20  for i = 1:length(g)
21      sigma = 0.65*g(i).Wavelength;
22      gabor_mag(:,:,i) = imgaussfilt(gabor_mag(:,:,i),3.5*sigma);
23  end
24
25  %--------------------------
26  % Supplement the information about each pixel with spatial location
27  % information. This additional information allows the k-means clustering
28  % algorithm to prefer groupings that are close together spatially.
29  % Get the x and y coordinates of all pixels in the input image.
30  n_rows = size(img_1,1);
31  n_cols = size(img_1,2);
```

```
32  [x,y] = meshgrid(1:n_cols,1:n_rows);
33
34  %---------------------------
35  % Concatenate intensity, texture, and spatial information about each pixel.
36  featureSet = cat(3,img_1_gray,gabor_mag,x,y);
37  % Segment the image into two regions using k-means clustering with
38  % the supplemented feature set.
39  labels = imsegkmeans(featureSet,2,'NormalizeInput',true);
40  labeled_image = labeloverlay(img_1,labels);
41  imshow(labeled_image)
42  title('Labeled Image with Additional Pixel Information')
43
44  montage({img_1, labeled_image})
```

Listing 20.4 shows a clever solution to the problem. It illustrates how to combine intensity (converting the image from RGB to gray), local texture (via Gabor filters), and location information (using a mesh grid) to successfully segment the foreground object from the background[5]. The result (Figure 20.4(b)) is quite good if compared to the first attempt (Listing 20.3 and Figure 20.3).

Discussion (Recipe notes)

In this recipe, you learned how to use the k-means clustering algorithm to quantize pixels according to their colors or intensities. In its simplest form,

(a)   (b)

FIGURE 20.4
Successful attempt at image segmentation using k-means clustering augmented with intensity, texture, and spatial location information: (a) original image; (b) segmented image.

and for images with "easy" objects and uncomplicated texture, this can provide a quick way to group regions of similar color (e.g., for visualization purposes).

We also learned that in order to use the `imsegkmeans` MATLAB function to perform proper segmentation, additional preprocessing is needed to convey supplementary information (features), such as intensity, texture, and spatial information.

At this point, if you think there should be better segmentation algorithms out there, you are correct. We will see some of them in upcoming recipes.

Learn more about it

Useful MATLAB functions

Type the function name in the search field at www.mathworks.com/help/matlab/
· `imsegkmeans` · `label2rgb` · `labeloverlay` · `rgb2lab` ·

MATLAB documentation, demos, and examples

- Color-Based Segmentation Using K-Means Clustering
  www.mathworks.com/help/images/color-based-segmentation-using-k-means-clustering.html

- Texture Segmentation Using Gabor Filters
  www.mathworks.com/help/images/texture-segmentation-using-gabor-filters.html

Notes

1 This can be useful in some cases, as you will see in Part 1 of this recipe.
2 You will learn how to do it in Part 2 of this recipe.
3 The attentive reader will probably remember that Recipe 14 taught some ideas on how to solve the uneven illumination problem that might help in these cases. Since we are dealing with color images, a more elegant solution will be to decouple luminance from chrominance, as you will see later in this recipe.
4 Making K = 7 will partially solve the problem by grouping the black pixels belonging to the marker into their own cluster, separate from any other cluster that maps to chip colors. Try it!
5 This example was adapted from the official documentation page for `imsegkmeans` (listed in the *Learn more about it* section). Please check the source for additional details.

21

Recipe 21: Superpixel oversegmentation using SLIC

This recipe teaches you to perform superpixel image oversegmentation using the popular SLIC (Simple Linear Iterative Clustering) technique.

Superpixel oversegmentation is a technique that groups pixels in an image into compact and perceptually meaningful regions. This technique can help reduce the complexity of an image by representing it with a smaller set of regions while preserving the essential features. It is often used as an intermediate approach in the segmentation process[1].

One approach to superpixel oversegmentation is SLIC, which stands for Simple Linear Iterative Clustering. The SLIC algorithm uses k-means clustering[2] to group pixels in the image based on color similarity and spatial proximity. The algorithm takes as input the desired number of superpixels and iteratively adjusts the position and color of the cluster centers until convergence. The SLIC algorithm is computationally efficient, and the resulting superpixels have compact shapes, well-defined boundaries, and consistent size.

You will need (Ingredients)

- MATLAB R2016a or later
- MATLAB Image Processing Toolbox (IPT) version R2016a or later
- (OPTIONAL[3]) One or more of your images

DOI: 10.1201/9781003170198-27

Steps (Preparation)

1. Load a color image into the workspace.
2. Compute the superpixels of the image using the `superpixels` function.
3. Display the superpixel boundaries overlaid on the original image and (visually) evaluate the quality of the results.

LISTING 21.1
Superpixel oversegmentation using SLIC.

```
1  % Superpixel oversegmentation using SLIC
2
3  img = imread('lighthouse.png');
4
5  % Compute superpixels of the image for 4 different values
6  for number_superpixels = [100 200 500 1000]
7      [label_matrix, ~] = superpixels(img, number_superpixels);
8      % Show superpixels overlaid on image
9      boundary_mask = boundarymask(label_matrix);
10     figure, imshow(imoverlay(img,boundary_mask,'yellow'))
11 end
12
13 % Play with 'compactness' argument
14 number_superpixels = 500;
15 for compactness_value = [1 10 15 20]
16     [label_matrix, ~] = superpixels(img, number_superpixels, ...
17         Method="slic", Compactness=compactness_value);
18     % Show superpixels overlaid on image
19     boundary_mask = boundarymask(label_matrix);
20     figure, imshow(imoverlay(img,boundary_mask,'yellow'))
21 end
```

Listing 21.1 illustrates how to perform superpixel oversegmentation using SLIC in MATLAB. It explores two aspects that might have an impact on the quality of the results:

1. The desired number of superpixels[4]. The loop in lines 6–11 calls the `superpixels` function with four different values for the `number_superpixels` argument (see Figure 21.1).
2. The `Compactness` argument. This parameter controls the *shape* of superpixels: higher values make superpixels more regularly shaped, i.e., square-like; lower values make superpixels adhere to boundaries better, making them irregularly shaped[5]. The loop in lines 15–21 calls the `superpixels` function with four different values (for a fixed number of 500 desired superpixels), whose results appear in Figure 21.2.

FIGURE 21.1
Results of applying superpixel oversegmentation using SLIC to the lighthouse image specifying different values for the desired number of superpixels: (a) 100; (b) 200; (c) 500; (d) 1000.

Discussion (Recipe notes)

In this recipe, you learned how to perform superpixel oversegmentation using SLIC in MATLAB using the superpixels function and experiment with
some of its arguments. This method can also be used for 3D images. See
useful references next.

FIGURE 21.2
Results of applying superpixel oversegmentation using SLIC to the lighthouse image with a fixed number of 500 desired superpixels and specifying different values for Compactness parameter: (a) 1; (b) 10; (c) 15; (d) 20.

Learn more about it

Useful MATLAB functions

Type the function name in the search field at www.mathworks.com/help/matlab/

`·superpixels·superpixels3·`

MATLAB documentation, demos, and examples

- Image Segmentation
  www.mathworks.com/help/images/image-segmentation.html
- Image Segmentation and Analysis
  www.mathworks.com/help/images/image-analysis.html
- Plot Land Classification with Color Features and Superpixels
  www.mathworks.com/help/images/land-classification-with-color-features-and-superpixels.html

---

Notes

1 See Recipe 22.
2 See Recipe 20.
3 The recipe has been prepared using MATLAB's built-in images.
4 Note that the `superpixels` function returns two variables: a label matrix and the *actual* number of superpixels computed. In Listing 21.1, we have no use for the latter and replaced it with a ∼. You might want to assign it to a variable and inspect its value to see how close it gets to the desired number of regions passed as an argument to the function.
5 Note that to keep `Compactness` constant during clustering, the `Method` argument has to be set to `slic` instead of the default, `slic0` (see lines 16–17).

22

Recipe 22: Graph-based segmentation

This recipe teaches you how to perform graph-based image segmentation in MATLAB.

Graph-based image segmentation techniques approach the problem of dividing an image into multiple segments or regions from the perspective of graph theory: the pixels in an image are represented as nodes, and the relationships between them are represented as edges. The goal of graph-based image segmentation is to find the optimal partitioning of an image into segments such that the pixels within each segment are as similar as possible and the pixels in different segments are as dissimilar as possible. This can be achieved by finding a minimum cut in the graph.

There are several graph-based algorithms in the literature. This recipe focuses on two of the most popular methods: GrabCut and lazy snapping.

- **GrabCut** combines interactive and automatic techniques to achieve high-quality image segmentation. It is an iterative process that starts with an initial estimation of the foreground and background regions and then uses graph-based optimization to refine this estimation. The algorithm is called "GrabCut" because it is designed to allow the user to "grab" the desired foreground object by providing a rough bounding box around it.

- **Lazy snapping** provides an interactive and efficient way of partitioning an image into multiple segments. The algorithm is called "lazy" because it does not require a full computation of the graph and instead only computes the necessary portions of the graph during the interactive process. In lazy snapping, the user provides *seed points* or *scribbles* to indicate the desired partition of the image, which will serve as the initial constraints for the segmentation process.

These algorithms are implemented by the `grabcut` and `lazysnapping` functions, respectively, available in MATLAB's Image Processing Toolbox.

DOI: 10.1201/9781003170198-28

You will need (Ingredients)

- MATLAB R2018a or later
- MATLAB Image Processing Toolbox (IPT) version R2018a or later
- Image file: `pinkphone.png`

Steps (Preparation)

Option 1: GrabCut

1. Load the image into the workspace.
2. Generate label matrix using the `superpixels` function[1]
3. Specify a region of interest (ROI) (enclosing the foreground objects), e.g., using `drawpolygon` and `poly2mask`.
4. Perform the GrabCut operation using the `grabcut` function, specifying the original image, the label matrix, and the ROI mask.
5. Display *before* and *after* images and (visually) evaluate the quality of the results.

Listing 22.1 illustrates how to segment the foreground object (a smartphone in a pink cover) from the background[2] using the `grabcut` function. The SLIC superpixel oversegmentation using the `superpixels` function (lines 5–6) is an intermediate step, and the resulting `label_matrix` is used as one of the parameters expected by the `grabcut` function (line 28).

Figure 22.1 shows intermediate images and final results. Note that there are some errors in both directions, i.e., some background (BG) pixels have been mistakenly labeled as foreground (FG) and vice-versa, which can be seen clearly in parts (c) and (d) of the figure. In Figure 22.2, when we take a closer look at some of the errors (zooming into the bottom-left portion of the phone case), the impact of the SLIC step becomes apparent: the segmentation errors are aligned with the superpixels' boundaries. In other words, this algorithm doesn't label *individual* pixels as either FG or BG but entire pixel regions (i.e., *superpixels*) instead.

LISTING 22.1

Segmentation using GrabCut.

```
1  % Segmentation using GrabCut
2  img = imread('pinkphone.png'); % Read image
3
4  % Compute superpixels of the image
5  number_superpixels = 500;
6  [label_matrix, number_labels] = superpixels(img, number_superpixels);
7
8  % Show superpixels overlaid on image
9  boundary_mask = boundarymask(label_matrix);
10 figure, imshow(imoverlay(img,boundary_mask,'yellow'))
11
12 % Specify a region of interest and create a mask image.
13 figure, imshow(img)
14
15 % Mode 1: interactive
16 % user will click and select vertices
17 % roi = drawpolygon("Color",'yellow');
18
19 % Mode 2: programmatic
20 % using coordinates of previously selected vertices
21 roi = drawpolygon('Position',[318,87; 1053,118; 1039,1828; 205,1804]);
22
23 roi_vertices = roi.Position;
24 roi_mask = poly2mask(roi_vertices(:,1),roi_vertices(:,2), ...
25     size(label_matrix,1),size(label_matrix,2));
26
27 % Apply GrabCut to image passing superpixels and ROI mask as arguments
28 mask = grabcut(img,label_matrix,roi_mask);
29 figure, imshow(mask)
30
31 % Create and display masked image
32 masked_image = img;
33 masked_image(repmat(~mask,[1 1 3])) = 0;
34 figure, imshow(masked_image)
35
36 % Create and display overlay image
37 overlay_image = labeloverlay(img, mask, 'Colormap',[0 1 0]);
38 figure, imshow(overlay_image)
39
40 % Create and display overlay image
41 overlay_image = img;
42 overlay_image(~mask) = 0.2*img(~mask);
43 figure, imshow(overlay_image)
```

The code in Listing 22.1 uses the coordinates of a polygon whose vertices have been programmatically selected (line 21) but has provision for being used in *interactive mode* using the drawpolygon function: you just need to uncomment line 17 and comment out line 21.

Option 2: Lazy snapping

1. Load the image into the workspace.

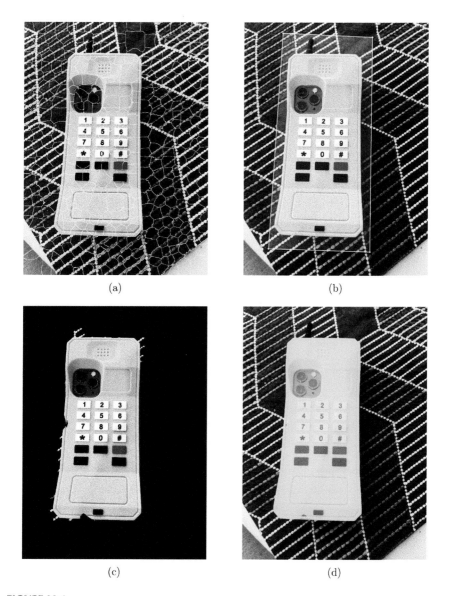

FIGURE 22.1
Image segmentation using GrabCut: (a) superpixel boundaries (yellow) overlaid on the input image; (b) selected polygon; (c) masked image; (d) overlay image.

2. Generate label matrix using the `superpixels` function.

3. Specify one or more rectangular ROIs denoting the foreground, using `drawrectangle` and `createmask`.

4. Specify one or more rectangular ROIs denoting the background, using `drawrectangle` and `createmask`.

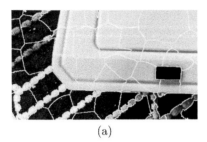 

(a)   (b)

FIGURE 22.2
A closer look at some errors: (a) superpixel boundaries (cyan) overlaid on the input image;
(b) overlay image.

5. Perform the lazy snapping operation using the `lazysnapping` function, specifying the original image, the label matrix, and the FG and
   BG ROIs.
6. Display *before* and *after* images and (visually) evaluate the quality of
   the results.

Listing 22.2 illustrates how to segment the foreground object from the background using the `lazysnapping` function and the same test image from
before.

Once again, the SLIC superpixel oversegmentation using the `superpix-
els` function (lines 5–6) appears as an intermediate step, and the resulting
`label_matrix` is used as one of the parameters expected by the `lazys-
napping` function (line 32).

In Listing 22.2, we also illustrate that the `lazysnapping` function supports multiple disjoint ROIs for specifying the background[3]. In this example,
these ROIs are created programmatically as three separate rectangles (lines
20–25), eventually combined into a single BG mask (lines 27–29).

Figure 22.3 shows intermediate images and final results. The FG and BG
masks appear as green and red rectangles, respectively, in part (b) of the
figure. Once again, there are some errors in both directions, i.e., some background pixels have been mistakenly labeled as foreground and vice-versa,
which can be seen clearly in parts (c) and (d) of the figure. The errors
are more pronounced than the ones obtained using the GrabCut algorithm
(Figure 22.1) for the same image. This might be due to the number of superpixel regions passed as an argument to the `superpixels` function (line 5)
as well the number, shape, location, and size of the FG and BG masks[4].

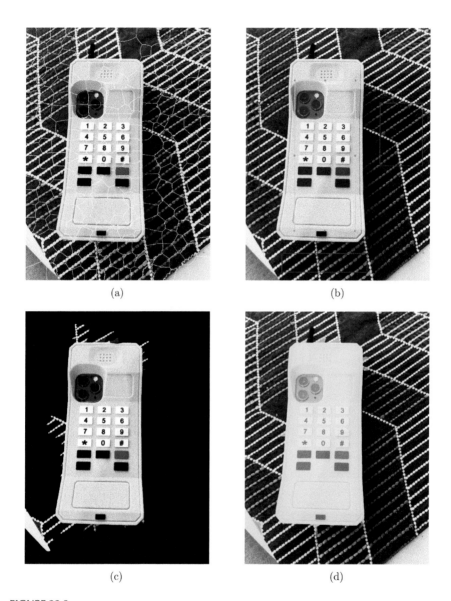

FIGURE 22.3
Image segmentation using lazy snapping: (a) superpixel boundaries (yellow) overlaid on the input image; (b) selected regions of interest (ROIs) for FG (green) and BG (red); (c) masked image; (d) overlay image.

LISTING 22.2
Segmentation using lazy snapping.

```
% Segmentation using lazy snapping
img = imread('pinkphone.png'); % Read image

% Compute superpixels of the image
number_superpixels = 300;
[label_matrix, number_labels] = superpixels(img, number_superpixels);

% Show superpixels overlaid on image
boundary_mask = boundarymask(label_matrix);
figure, imshow(imoverlay(img,boundary_mask,'yellow'))

% Specify foreground region of interest (ROI) and create foreground mask
figure, imshow(img)

foreground_roi = drawrectangle(gca,'Position',[400 420 500 1200], ...
    'Color','g');
foreground_mask = createMask(foreground_roi,img);

% Specify 1+ background ROIs and create corresponding masks
background_roi_1 = drawrectangle(gca,'Position',[1100 600 350 500], ...
    'Color','r'); % right side of the image
background_roi_2 = drawrectangle(gca,'Position',[10 600 100 700], ...
    'Color','r'); % left side of the image
background_roi_3 = drawrectangle(gca,'Position',[300 1800 700 150], ...
    'Color','r'); % bottom of the image

background_mask = createMask(background_roi_1,img) + ...
    createMask(background_roi_2,img) + ...
    createMask(background_roi_3,img);

% Apply lazy snapping to image passing superpixels and masks as arguments
mask = lazysnapping(img, label_matrix, foreground_mask, background_mask);
figure, imshow(mask)

% Create and display masked image
masked_image = img;
masked_image(repmat(~mask,[1 1 3])) = 0;
figure, imshow(masked_image)

% Create and display overlay image
overlay_image = labeloverlay(img, mask, 'Colormap',[0 1 0]);
figure, imshow(overlay_image)
```

Discussion (Recipe notes)

In this recipe, you learned how to perform graph-based image segmentation in MATLAB, using the `lazysnapping` and `grabcut` functions available in the Image Processing Toolbox. Both methods can be used for 3D images (see MATLAB documentation for examples).

You are encouraged to modify the examples in this recipe to investigate the impact of several parameters on the final result, such as the number of superpixels and the size and shape of the foreground and background ROIs.

Graph-based segmentation can also be performed interactively using the *Image Segmenter* App, which allows users to refine the algorithm's understanding of which pixels belong to foreground or background by using scribbles and interactively watching the results improve. We encourage you to give it a try!

Learn more about it

Useful MATLAB functions

Type the function name in the search field at www.mathworks.com/help/matlab/

· boundarymask · createMask · drawpolygon · drawrectangle ·grabcut·labeloverlay·lazysnapping·poly2mask·superpixels·

MATLAB documentation, demos, and examples

- Getting Started with Image Segmenter App
  www.mathworks.com/help/images/image-segmentation-using-the-image-segmenter-app.html

- Image Segmentation and Analysis
  www.mathworks.com/help/images/image-analysis.html

- Segment Image Using Local Graph Cut (Grabcut) in Image Segmenter
  www.mathworks.com/help/images/segment-image-using-local-graph-cut-grab-cut.html

---

Notes

1 See Recipe 21 for more details on superpixel oversegmentation using SLIC.
2 Note that the image has a textured background that would make earlier approaches, such as active contour and k-means clustering produce unacceptable results.
3 The grabcut function also supports multiple ROIs to indicate FG and BG masks.
4 You might want to change the code in Listing 22.2 to change the value in line 5 and make the BG masks bigger, especially the one at the bottom of the image, to see if it leads to improved results. The 'Position' name-value argument of drawrectangle function requires the rectangle position and size as $[x\ y\ w\ h]$, where x and y specify the upper left corner, and w and h specify the width and height.

Part VII

Binary image analysis

Part VII – Binary image analysis

A typical image processing workflow often requires the manipulation of binary images, either as a means to an end (e.g., producing binary masks for ROI-based image processing) or as an end by itself (e.g., counting, measuring, and identifying foreground objects and their properties).

The recipes in Part VII cover some of the most useful techniques for processing and analyzing binary images.

Recipe 23 teaches how to identify and manage individual connected components in a binary image. It guides you through the process of finding, counting, and accessing these components for subsequent analysis or examination.

Recipe 24 introduces the most popular morphological operations for binary images, and shows examples of their usage.

Recipe 25 teaches you how to compute region-based features for each connected component in a binary image. This information can be used to feed a machine learning algorithm to perform image classification.

23

Recipe 23: Finding, counting, and accessing connected components in binary images

---

This recipe teaches how to identify and manage individual connected components in a binary image. It walks you through the process of finding, counting, and accessing these components for subsequent analysis or examination.

You will need (Ingredients)

- MATLAB R2009a or later
- MATLAB Image Processing Toolbox (IPT) version R2009a or later
- Image file: `bean_coffee_08.png`

Steps (Preparation)

1. Load a binary input image, or binarize it using one of the techniques in Recipe 18.
2. Use `bwconncomp` to locate, count, and access the connected components.
3. Use `labelmatrix` and `label2rgb` to show the identified connected components.

Connected components in a binary image are clusters of pixels that often correspond to objects or regions of interest within the image. Listing 23.1 demonstrates the successful separation of the background and the coffee beans, which are the objects of interest, using global thresholding with Otsu's method, originally introduced in Recipe 18.

DOI: 10.1201/9781003170198-30

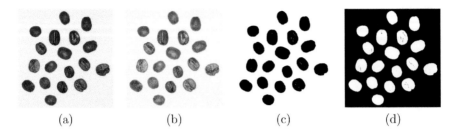

      (a)   (b)   (c)   (d)

FIGURE 23.1
Binarization of image to obtain the connected components corresponding to the coffee beans. (a) Original image; (b) grayscale version; (c) after binarization; (d) complement of binarized image.

LISTING 23.1
Foreground-background segmentation using global thresholding.

```
1  % Segmentation using global thresholding
2  img_1 = imread ('bean_coffee_08.png');
3  figure, imshow(img_1), title('Input')
4  img_1_g = rgb2gray(img_1);
5  level = graythresh(img_1_g);
6  img_1_bw = imbinarize(img_1_g, level);
7  figure, montage ({img_1_g, img_1_bw}), title('Grayscale, binary')
8  img_1_bw = ~img_1_bw;
9  figure, imshow(img_1_bw), title('Connected components')
10 imwrite(img_1_bw, 'bean_coffee_08_bw.png') %save 1 bit per pixel image
```

Figure 23.1 shows the most relevant results. Note that the coffee beans are dark objects over a light background, so we complement the binary image to obtain a final representation, shown in part (d), where the white (logical one or "true") pixels correspond to the desired connected components and the black (logical zero or "false") to the background.

Once a binary image containing one or more connected components of interest has been produced, we can use the MATLAB function bwconncomp to take the binary image as input and output a structure (stored in variable CC in Listing 23.2) that contains the following fields:

- Connectivity: this parameter is the neighborhood that specifies whether a pixel is part of the same connected component. For 2D images, it can be 4 (the four adjacent neighbors of a pixel) or 8 (the eight neighbors of a pixel). The default value is 8.
- ImageSize: size of the input binary image.
- NumObjects: the number of connected components detected by the function.
- PixelIdxList: a cell array containing the connected components themselves, organized as follows: each element of the array stores a vector with the linear indices of the pixels belonging to that connected component.

In Listing 23.2, we use `bwconncomp` to find and count the coffee beans in the image. As expected, the obtained `NumObjects` is 18.

LISTING 23.2
Finding and counting connected components.

```
% Find and count connected components
img_1_bw = imread ('bean_coffee_08_bw.png');
figure, imshow(img_1_bw), title('Input')
CC = bwconncomp(img_1_bw);
disp(['Number of connected components: ' num2str(CC.NumObjects)])
img_1_bw(CC.PixelIdxList{7}) = 0;
figure, imshow(img_1_bw), title('Excluding connected component 7')
```

Typing `CC` in the Command Window to inspect its content, you should get:

```
CC =
   struct with fields:
      Connectivity: 8
        ImageSize: [500 500]
       NumObjects: 18
      PixelIdxList: {1x18 cell}
```

To illustrate how to access the `PixelIdxList` field, the code in line 6 of Listing 23.2 excludes an arbitrarily chosen connected component (number 7, in this case) from the image. The result is shown in Figure 23.2.

The conventional method for distinguishing connected components in image processing is commonly known as *region labeling*. When provided with a binary image as input, a labeling algorithm generates an output image of the same dimensions, assigning a consistent label to each pixel belonging to a connected component. The labels are numbered from 1 to n, where n represents the total count of connected components.

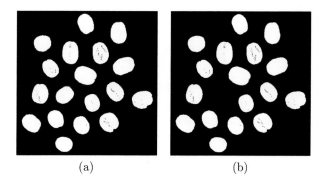

(a)   (b)

FIGURE 23.2
Excluding a connected component from the binary image. (a) Original binarized image; (b) output image, with one of the 18 connected components removed.

We can use MATLAB functions `labelmatrix` and `label2rgb` to visualize the connected components and their respective identifiers (*labels*) in an image, as demonstrated in Listing 23.3.

LISTING 23.3

Labeling connected components.

```
1 % Label connnected components
2 img_1_bw = imread ('bean_coffee_08_bw.png');
3 figure, imshow(img_1_bw), title('Input')
4 CC = bwconncomp(img_1_bw);
5 disp(['Number of connected components: ' num2str(CC.NumObjects)])
6 img_1_bw_L = labelmatrix(CC);
7 figure, h = imshow(img_1_bw_L, []); title('Labeled connected comp.')
8 img_1_bw_L_rgb = label2rgb(img_1_bw_L);
9 figure, imshow(img_1_bw_L_rgb), title('Labeled connected comp. pseudoc.')
```

The `labelmatrix` function takes the `CC` structure as input and labels every pixel of each connected component with its respective index, obtained from the cell array stored in the `PixelIdxList` field. With `label2rgb`, it is possible to pseudocolor the labeled image for clearer visualization (Figure 23.3).

Moreover, we can inspect the labels into the image with *Pixel Region* tool, typing:

```
impixelregion(h)
```

Figure 23.4 illustrates the process. It shows the pixel values (i.e., the labels for each connected component) for the first and last connected components. Figure 23.5 shows all connected components with their respective labels (in red text) overlaid.

When connected components touch the borders of the image, they might represent *incomplete* objects of interest in the original image. If necessary, you can exclude them from the image using the `imclearborder` function, as shown in the code in Listing 23.4, whose results appear in Figure 23.6.

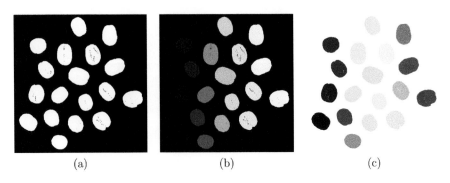

(a)   (b)   (c)

FIGURE 23.3

Connected components with their respective labels. (a) Input image; (b) grayscale image containing the labels; and (c) the final, pseudocolored version.

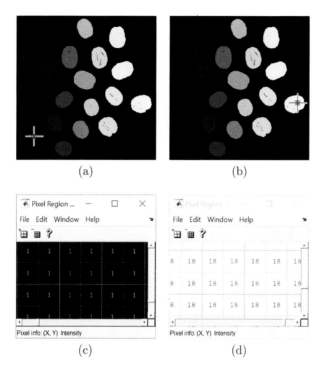

FIGURE 23.4
Inspecting labels using the `impixelregion` function: (a) and (c) first connected component (labeled as 1); (b) and (d) last connected component (labeled as 18).

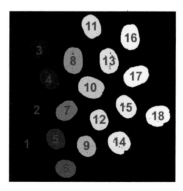

FIGURE 23.5
Labeled connected components.

The number of connected components for the original image, its central patch – extracted from the input image with the upper left corner at coordinates x and $y = 100$ and the bottom right corner at coordinates x and $y = 400$

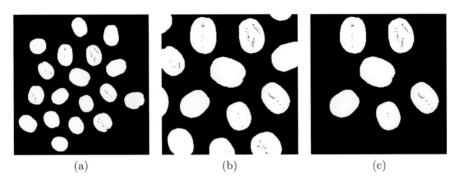

FIGURE 23.6
Excluding connected components linked to the borders of the image. (a) Original image; (b) central patch; (c) result of applying `imclearborder` to (b).

– and the same central patch after applying the `imclearborder` function are shown below:

```
Number of con. comp. Original: 18
Number of con. comp. Central patch: 14
Number of con. comp. Central patch borders cleared: 6
```

LISTING 23.4
Using `imclearborder` to remove connected components that touch the borders of the image.

```
1  % Clear borders
2  img_1_bw = imread ('bean_coffee_08_bw.png');
3  CC = bwconncomp(img_1_bw);
4  figure, imshow(img_1_bw), title('Original')
5
6  img_1_bw_p = img_1_bw(100:400,100:400);
7  CCp = bwconncomp(img_1_bw_p);
8  figure, imshow(img_1_bw_p), title('Central patch')
9  img_1_bw_pc = imclearborder(img_1_bw_p);
10 figure, imshow(img_1_bw_pc), title('Central patch borders cleared')
11 CCpc = bwconncomp(img_1_bw_pc);
12
13 disp(['Number of con. comp. Original: ' num2str(CC.NumObjects)])
14 disp(['Number of con. comp. Central patch: ' num2str(CCp.NumObjects)])
15 disp(['Number of con. comp. Central patch borders cleared: '...
16     num2str(CCpc.NumObjects)])
```

Discussion (Recipe notes)

In this recipe, you learned how to locate, enumerate, and analyze individual connected components in a binary image for subsequent processing or modification.

In our examples, the bwconncomp function outputs the connected components as sets of linear coordinates rather than an image representation. To generate an image with labeled components, the labelmatrix function can be utilized in conjunction with bwconncomp. Additionally, for improved visualization of the connected components, label2rgb can assign pseudocolors to the labeled image.

In MATLAB, you can also perform connected component labeling using the bwlabel function, which accepts the binary image as an input. However, in this recipe, we adopted labelmatrix due to its lower memory usage.

Learn more about it

Useful MATLAB functions

Type the function name in the search field at www.mathworks.com/help/matlab/
· bwconncomp · bwlabel · imclearborder · impixelregion · label2rgb · labelmatrix ·

MATLAB documentation, demos, and examples

- Label and Measure Connected Components in a Binary Image
  www.mathworks.com/help/images/label-and-measure-objects-in-a-binary-image.html
- Pixel Connectivity
  www.mathworks.com/help/images/pixel-connectivity.html

24

Recipe 24: Basic morphological operations

This recipe teaches you the definitions and interpretations of morphological operations such as *dilation, erosion, opening, closing* for binary images, along with methods for their application.

The term *morphology* is related to the form and structure of objects. In binary image processing, morphological operations can be used to analyze and manipulate the shapes of connected components (objects).

The idea is to probe every image pixel using a well-defined *structuring element* (SE), in which the morphological operation is applied. The shape and size of the SE can present any desired configuration, depending on the application, although regular shapes such as squares, diamonds, and disks are the most employed. The reference point of the SE is referred to *origin, central point*, or *center*. However, since it does not necessarily correspond to the geometric center, we adopt the term *hot spot* here.

When applying morphological operations to binary images, it is important to remember that – by convention – pixels belonging to foreground objects will have a value of 1 (white pixels), whereas background pixels will have a value of 0 (black pixels). The same convention is adopted for the SE, i.e., an active point has a value of 1, and an inactive (irrelevant, or "don't care") point has a value of 0.

The mathematical formulation of morphological operations predominantly uses set notation and can be found in various references, such as [18, 12]. For the sake of simplicity, in this recipe, we will present the definition of operations in a textual format.

You will need (Ingredients)

- MATLAB R2006a or later
- MATLAB Image Processing Toolbox (IPT) version R2006a or later
- Image files: `18x12_bw_1.png`, `250x250_bw_3cb.png`, `250x250_bw_3cb2_n.png`

DOI: 10.1201/9781003170198-31

Steps (Preparation)

Morphological operations in MATLAB usually follow these steps:

1. Load a binary input image, or binarize it using one of the techniques in Part VI.
2. Specify desired SE to actuate on the morphological operation(s) using `strel`.
3. Apply desired morphological operation(s) to the image using `imdilate`, `imerode`, `imopen`, `imclose`.
4. Display before and after images and interpret the results.

1: Primary operations: dilation and erosion

Dilation and *erosion*, as their names suggest, aim to add pixels to an image and remove pixels from an image, respectively. The SE's size, geometry, and position of the hot spot establish the effect of the dilation and erosion over the input image.

To define the operations, let's say that a binary input image A is submitted to dilation D or erosion E by a SE se. The output image D or E is initialized with A. The SE se visits every pixel of input A, and every time that the hot spot hs of se finds a 1 (white) pixel:

- **Dilation** of A by se, denoted by $D = A \oplus se$: the entire se is inserted in output image D.
- **Erosion** of A by se, denoted by $E = A \ominus se$: the hs of se is eliminated from output image E if se does not fit entirely into the object.

Figure 24.1 presents examples of dilation (part (a)) and erosion (part (b)) applied to a simple 18×12 binary image A, for easier inspection of the operations for every pixel. The SE se is an "inverted T", with hot spot hs at the horizontal line's center (identified by a black circle). The bold line at the outputs D and E represents the boundary of the connected components (objects) in the original image A.

In MATLAB, these morphological operations are implemented using `imdilate` and `imerode`. They work in association with the `strel` function, which creates the SE (an object of class `strel`).

Listing 24.1[1] reproduces the examples in Figure 24.1. To specify the arbitrary "inverted T" SE, the function `strel` receives a matrix with 1's and 0's (variable `nhood`), where 1 is an active, and 0 is an inactive (irrelevant, or "don't care") point of the SE. To position the hot spot of the SE at the center of the horizontal line of the "inverted T," an additional row of 0's is required

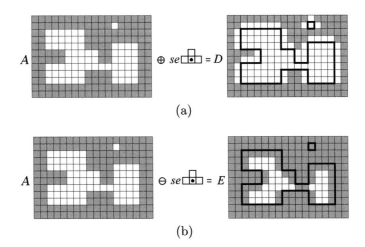

FIGURE 24.1
Example of morphological operations: (a) dilation of image *A* by structuring element *se* resulting in image *D*; (b) erosion of image *A* by the same SE resulting in image *E*.

(line 8) because the hot spot's position is given by floor(((size(nhood) + 1)/2), such that for a $M \times N$ matrix, with M and N odd numbers, the hot spot's position matches the geometrical center. Thus, for a 3×3 matrix nhood, the hot spot lies at position $(2, 2)$. Lines 10 to 12 of the code were included to illustrate the position of the hot spot with a black circle.

LISTING 24.1
Morphological dilation and erosion.

```
1  % Morphological Dilation and Erosion
2  bw = imread('18x12_bw_1.png');
3  figure, subplot(4,1,1)
4  imshow(bw), title('Input')
5  h_bw = impixelregion; set(h_bw,'Name','Input')
6  nhood = [ 0 1 0   % structuring element specification
7            1 1 1
8            0 0 0];
9  se = strel('arbitrary',nhood); % create the structuring element
10 se_hs = floor((size(nhood)+1)/2);
11 subplot(4,1,2), imshow(se.Neighborhood), title('SE')
12 hold on, plot(se_hs(1),se_hs(2),'ko','MarkerFaceColor','k'), hold off
13 % Dilation
14 bw_d = imdilate(bw,se);
15 subplot(4,1,3), imshow(bw_d), title('Dilation')
16 h_bw_d = impixelregion; set(h_bw_d,'Name','Dilation')
17 % Erosion
18 bw_e = imerode(bw,se);
19 subplot(4,1,4), imshow(bw_e), title('Erosion')
20 h_bw_e = impixelregion; set(h_bw_e,'Name','Erosion')
```

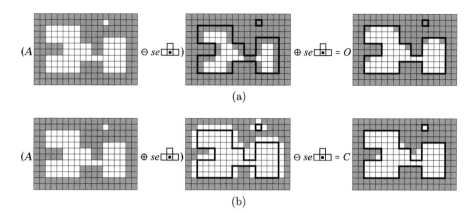

FIGURE 24.2
Example of morphological operations (a) opening of image A by SE se resulting in image O; (b) closing of image A by the same SE se resulting in image C.

2: Compound operations: opening and closing

Opening and *closing* are compound morphological operations derived from simple combinations of dilation and erosion and defined as follows:

- **Opening** of A by se, denoted by $O = A \circ se$: $O = (A \ominus se) \oplus se$, i.e., an erosion followed by dilation with the same SE, se.
- **Closing** of A by se, denoted by $C = A \bullet se$: $C = (A \oplus se) \ominus se$, i.e., a dilation followed by erosion with the same SE, se.

Figure 24.2 presents examples of opening (part (a)) and closing (part (b)) applied to the same image and using the same SE as in Figure 24.1 (which illustrates dilation and erosion). To reproduce this example in MATLAB you can start from the code in Listing 24.1 as a template and use `imopen` and `imclose` instead of `imdilate` and `imerode`.

These operations behave as follows: *opening* breaks narrow connections and eliminates thin protrusions; *closing* connects narrow breaks and fills small holes and gaps in contours. It is worth reinforcing that, to obtain such effects, the SE's size must be compatible with the mentioned elements' (connections, protrusions, breaks, gaps).

The code in Listing 24.2 applies these operations to a 250×250 pixel image containing binary objects corresponding to coffee beans. The original image is submitted to opening and closing with a predefined SE of `'disk'` shape, of radii $r = 3$, 4, and 5. To inspect a SE, after running the code, open the variable `se` to view its `Neighborhood` field, or type `se.Neighborhood` in the command line.

LISTING 24.2
Morphological opening and closing.

```
% Morphological Opening and Closing
bw = imread('250x250_bw_3cb.png');
h(1) = figure;
subplot(1,4,1), imshow(bw), title('Input')
h(2) = figure;
subplot(1,4,1), imshow(bw), title('Input')
p = 2;
for r = 3:5
    se = strel('disk',r); % create pre-defined structuring element
    bw_o = imopen(bw,se); % opening
    figure(h(1)), subplot(1,4,p), imshow(bw_o),...
        title(['Opening r=',num2str(r)])
    bw_c = imclose(bw,se); % closing
    figure(h(2)), subplot(1,4,p), imshow(bw_c),...
        title(['Closing r=',num2str(r)])
    p = p+1;
end
```

Figure 24.3 shows the results for opening and closing, where the leftmost image is the input (original), and the following are the outputs for $r = 3$, $r = 4$, $r = 5$. In the opening, an SE of $r = 3$ and $r = 4$ could eliminate the protrusion but not break the narrow connection, whereas an SE with $r = 5$ did. In closing, one can note that five of the six holes were filled with a SE

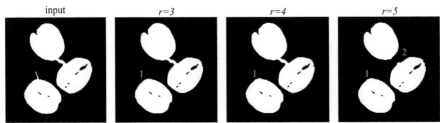

Opening - 1: eliminates thin protrusions; 2: breakes narrow connections

(a)

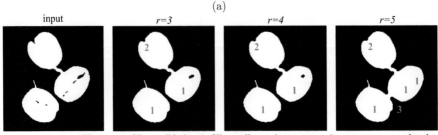

Closing - 1: fills small holes; 2: fills small gaps in contours; 3: connects narrow breaks

(b)

FIGURE 24.3
Example of morphological operations (a) opening and (b) closing, with a SE of disk shape and increasing radii of $r = 3$, $r = 4$, $r = 5$.

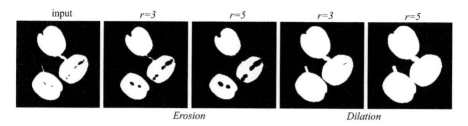

FIGURE 24.4
Example of applying morphological erosion and dilation with SEs of $r = 3$ and $r = 5$.

of $r \geqslant 3$. The larger hole was partially filled with $r = 3$ and $r = 4$, and completely filled with $r = 5$. The small gap in the top contour was gradually filled with the radius increasing. Finally, an $r = 5$ connected two objects that were apart.

Figure 24.4 presents the results of single erosion and dilation operations with SEs of $r = 3$ and $r = 5$. Compared with opening and closing, which tend to act on connections, protrusions, breaks, and gaps, one can note that erosion "retracts" entire objects, whereas dilation "grows" entire objects.

3: Open-close filter

Binary images often contain both the targeted objects of interest and unwanted connected components. These superfluous components can arise due to problems during image capture or the binarization process. Typically viewed as noise, these undesired elements often require removal. However, even the desired objects may have flaws, such as tiny holes or irregular edges. To refine images with these traits, we can apply a sequence of opening and closing operations. The opening operation effectively eliminates connected components smaller than the structuring element (SE), while the closing operation aids in bridging small gaps and smoothing out contours.

This morphological operation is known as *open-close filter* (a type of *morphological filter*). The open-close filtering of an input image A using a SE se, denoted by OC, is $OC = (A \circ se) \bullet se$, i.e., an opening followed by closing with the same SE, se.

The code in Listing 24.3 implements open-close filtering applied to a 250×250 pixel input image containing binary regions corresponding to coffee beans over a noisy background due to the presence of dirt particles. The SE se is a disk with radius $r = 5$. Results are shown in Figure 24.5. During the opening step, the noisy background was cleaned up, and after closing, small holes were filled.

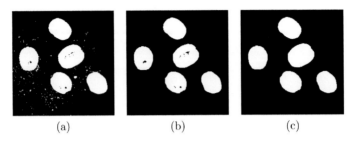

FIGURE 24.5
Open-close filtering using a SE of disk shape with radius $r = 5$. (a) Input image; (b) opening; (c) subsequent closing.

LISTING 24.3
Morphological open-close filter.

```
1  % Mophological filtering (open-close filter)
2  bw = imread('250x250_bw_3cb2_n.png');
3  se = strel('disk', 5);
4  bw_o = imopen(bw,se); % opening of input image
5  bw_o_c = imclose(bw_o,se); % closing of opened image
6  subplot(1,3,1), imshow(bw), title('Input')
7  subplot(1,3,2), imshow(bw_o), title('open(Input)')
8  subplot(1,3,3), imshow(bw_o_c), title('close(open(Input))')
```

4: Designing your structuring elements

The `strel` function allows the creation of any desired SE. The user can manually define arbitrary SEs or ask for pre-defined shapes: diamond, octagon, disk, line, square, rectangle. Figure 24.6 presents examples of these SEs obtained with `strel` function. The code snippets in the figure show that the logical matrices containing the SEs *per se* are stored in `se.Neighborhood`.

5: Going further with `bwmorph`

Several other morphological processing techniques can be found in MATLAB. Listing 24.4 shows how to use the `bwmorph` function to implement *skeletonization*, a process that gradually wears away structures until they are only 1 pixel thick, without breaking them apart, and *thickening* to thicken objects without connecting previously unconnected ones.

The `imfill` function performs *region filling* and is useful to fill holes into the objects. The `bwperim` function extracts the *perimeter of objects* (boundary). Figure 24.7 presents the results. The original image (a) is submitted to a hole filling (b). Then, the filled image (b) is processed with skeletonization (c), thickening (d), and perimeter extraction (e).

r = 6;
se = strel('diamond',r);
se.Neighborhood

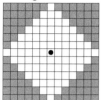

r = 6;
se = strel('octagon',r);
se.Neighborhood

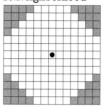

r = 6;
se = strel('disk',r);
se.Neighborhood

len = 7; deg = 0;
se = strel('line',len,deg);
se.Neighborhood

w = 7;
se = strel('square',w);
se.Neighborhood

m = 5; n = 7;
se = strel('rectangle',[m n]);
se.Neighborhood

FIGURE 24.6
Examples of pre-defined SEs obtained with strel function.

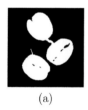    

   (a)   (b)   (c)   (d)   (e)

FIGURE 24.7
Morphological techniques obtained with imfill, bwmorph, and bwperim functions. (a) Original image; (b) original image with filled holes; (c) skeleton of (b); (d) thickening of (b); (e) perimeter extraction of (b).

LISTING 24.4
Additional morphological techniques.

```
% Other morphological techniques
bw = imread('250x250_bw_3cb.png');
subplot(2,4,1), imshow(bw), title('Original');
bw_f = imfill(bw,'holes'); % holes filling
subplot(2,4,2), imshow(bw_f), title('Filled');
bw_f_s = bwmorph(bw_f,'skel',Inf); % skeletonization
subplot(2,4,6), imshow(bw_f_s), title('Skeleton of Filled');
bw_f_t = bwmorph(bw_f,'thicken',5); % thickening
subplot(2,4,7), imshow(bw_f_t), title('Thickening of Filled');
bw_f_p = bwperim(bw_f); % perimeter extracting
subplot(2,4,8), imshow(bw_f_p), title('Perimeter of Filled');
```

Discussion (Recipe notes)

In this recipe, you learned the definitions and how to interpret and apply the basic (dilation, erosion) and compound (opening, closing) morphological operations, including the open-close filter.

Morphological image processing is a vast topic with extensive support in MATLAB. The bwmorph function alone provides many other operations worth exploring.

Learn more about it

Useful MATLAB functions

Type the function name in the search field at www.mathworks.com/help/matlab/
 · bwmorph · bwperim · imclose · imdilate · imerode · imfill · imopen · strel ·

MATLAB documentation, demos, and examples

- Binary Morphology in Image Processing (MathWorks Teaching Resources)
  www.mathworks.com/matlabcentral/fileexchange/94590-binary-morphology-in-image-processing
- Morphological Operations
  www.mathworks.com/help/images/morphological-filtering.html
- Structuring Elements
  www.mathworks.com/help/images/structuring-elements.html
- Types of Morphological Operations
  www.mathworks.com/help/images/morphological-dilation-and-erosion.html

Note

1 You are encouraged to run the code and confirm the results!

25

Recipe 25: Computing connected components' features

This recipe teaches you how to compute region-based features of the connected components in a binary image using the `regionprops` function available in the MATLAB Image Processing Toolbox.

When processing binary images, one key concept is the identification and analysis of "connected components" within those images. At its core, a *connected component* is a set of neighboring pixels in a binary image that share the same value, typically '1' or 'true', indicating they belong to the same object or region. These components provide an essential means to separate and identify individual objects within an image, especially when multiple objects are present.

Once connected components are identified, MATLAB's `regionprops` function becomes a valuable tool, allowing users to compute a myriad of properties associated with each component. These properties range from basic ones like `'Area'`, indicating the number of pixels in the component, to more complex descriptors like `'Centroid'`, specifying the center of mass of the component, or `'BoundingBox'`, which provides the smallest rectangle encompassing the component. Other properties such as `'Perimeter'`, `'Eccentricity'`, and `'Orientation'` can offer insights into the shape and orientation of the object. From these properties, one can glean significant information about the objects.

The following example illustrates the application of connected components' features into the usual "segmentation → feature extraction → classification" image processing pipeline. Figure 25.1(a), top part, shows an image containing three types of balls – *toy*, *American football*, and *tennis*, – on a regular background. Figure 25.1(a), bottom part, shows the image segmented with MATLAB's *Image Segmenter* App[1]. Using the segmented image, we can extract features from the corresponding connected components and use them for the subsequent classification of the objects. Figure 25.1(b) shows the values of the selected features – *eccentricity* (between 0 and 1) and *area* (in pixels) – to discriminate the three categories of sports balls, using elementary rules as shown in Figure 25.1(c). The *eccentricity* values can be used to distinguish

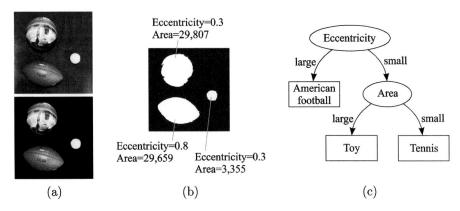

FIGURE 25.1
A simple example of the usual pipeline "segmentation → feature extraction → classification" in image processing. (a) Top: input image with three types of balls – toy, tennis, and American football, bottom: segmented image; (b) values of *eccentricity* and *area* features of the connected components corresponding to the balls; (c) simple rules based on the selected features to classify the objects.

spherical balls from the American football one, whereas the *area* is adequate to distinguish the toy ball from the tennis ball in the image.

Eccentricity and area are just two of the many features that can be used to describe the properties of connected components in binary images. In this recipe, we use MATLAB's `regionprops` function to explore many other region-based features that describe connected components.

You will need (Ingredients)

- MATLAB R2019a or later
- MATLAB Image Processing Toolbox (IPT) version R2019a or later
- Image files: `lego_23_c500.png` and `sball_4_matseglgc3b.png`

Steps (Preparation)

1. Load a binary input image, or binarize a color/grayscale image using one of the techniques in Part VI.
2. Specify desired connected components' features to be computed.
3. Compute the features using `regionprops`.
4. Visualize features' values in table format or superimpose them on the image.

Listing 25.1 explores the input/output options of the `regionprops` function, using the example image and features of Figure 25.1. The input can be a binary image, a `CC` struct (see Recipe 23), or a labeled image, i.e., an image with the labels of the connected components (see Recipe 23). The output is stored in a variable of class `table`[2] or into an array of structures. In addition to *eccentricity* and *area*, we also compute the *centroid* of the objects (line 16) which will be used to position (line 21) the identifying labels overlaid on the original image (with "1" over the American football, "2" over the toy ball, and "3" over the tennis ball). The nth element of the array of structures `f_s` stores the features of the object n. Thus, the toy ball's features, for example, are accessed with `f_s(2)`.

LISTING 25.1
Experimenting with some of the input/output options of the `regionprops` function.

```
1  % Function regionprops input/output
2  bw = imread('sball_4_matseglgc3b.png');
3
4  % Input: binary image, Output: table
5  f_t_1 = regionprops("table",bw,"Eccentricity","Area");
6  % Input: CC struct, Output: table
7  cc = bwconncomp(bw);
8  f_t_2 = regionprops("table",cc,"Eccentricity","Area");
9  % Input: labeled image, Output: table
10 bw_L = labelmatrix(cc);
11 f_t_3 = regionprops("table",bw_L,"Eccentricity","Area");
12
13 disp(['Equal outputs: ' num2str(isequal(f_t_1,f_t_2,f_t_3))])
14
15 % Input: binary image, Output: structure array
16 f_s = regionprops(bw,"Eccentricity","Area","Centroid");
17 figure, imshow(bw)
18 % Show the label (number) of the object on the image
19 hold on
20 for n=1:length(f_s) % stats_s(n) is the nth object
21     text(f_s(n).Centroid(1),f_s(n).Centroid(2),num2str(n),'Color','red')
22 end
23 hold off
```

Typing `f_t_1` and `f_s` in the command window, you can view the outputs of types `table` and array of structures, respectively:

```
f_t_1 =
  3×2 table
    Area       Eccentricity

    29659        0.79528
    29807        0.27479
     3355        0.29585


f_s =
  3×1 struct array with fields:
    Area
    Centroid
    Eccentricity
```

The `regionprops` function can measure several features from the connected components. It is worth mentioning that MATLAB's `regionprops` documentation employs the term *property* to refer to a feature, and *region* to refer to a connected component. In the following sections, features (input parameter `properties` for the `regionprops` function) are grouped according to different criteria for a better organization.

1: Features of *scalar* type

In this group of features, we present those that output a scalar (single number).

- `"Area"`: area of the region in pixels.
- `"Circularity"`: or roundness given by

$$C = \frac{4\pi A}{P^2} \left(1 - \frac{0.5}{r}\right)^2$$

  where A is the area, P the perimeter and $r = P/2\pi + 0.5$.
- `"ConvexArea"`: area in pixels of `"ConvexImage"` feature[3].
- `"Eccentricity"`: or elongation, defined by $E = $ ratio of the distance between the foci of an ellipse (that has the same second moments as the region) and its major axis length. $0 \leqslant E \leqslant 1$; $E = 0$ for a circle; $E = 1$ for a line.
- `"EquivDiameter"`: diameter of a circle that has the same area as the region, calculated by

$$E_d = \sqrt{\frac{4A}{\pi}}$$

- `"EulerNumber"`: 1 minus the number of holes within the region.
- `"Extent"`: quotient between the region's area and its bounding box's area.
- `"FilledArea"`: area in pixels of `"FilledImage"` feature[3].
- `"MajorAxisLength"`: major axis length of an ellipse, where the ellipse's normalized second central moments is the same as the region[4].
- `"MinorAxisLength"`: minor axis length of an ellipse, where the ellipse's normalized second central moments is the same as the region[5].
- `"Orientation"`: angle θ in degrees ($-90° \leqslant \theta \leqslant 90°$) between the horizontal axis ($0°$) and the major axis of an ellipse, where the ellipse's second moments is the same as the region[6]. By convention, positive angles indicate counterclockwise orientation, whereas negative angles mean clockwise.
- `"Perimeter"`: length of the outer border of the region.

- "Solidity": quotient between the region's area and its convex hull's[7] area, obtained by "Area"/"ConvexArea".

In Listing 25.2 we compute the above features for a color input image containing four Lego pieces.

The image is segmented following these steps (lines 4–9):

(i) Color to grayscale conversion (Recipe 26);

(ii) Gaussian filtering with $\sigma = 2$ to smooth internal noise to the objects, mainly significantly brighter spots due to the illumination, and eventual noise in the background (Recipe 15);

(iii) Global automatic thresholding using Otsu's method (Recipe 18);

(iv) Inverting the resulting binary image to produce an output in which white pixels correspond to objects and black pixels to the background (Recipe 23).

The resulting binary image with the segmented objects is saved into the lego_23_c500_bw.png file (line 29).

Figure 25.2 presents the results, including the values of the computed features.

LISTING 25.2
Computing features of *scalar* type with regionprops function.

```
1  % Function regionprops, features of scalar type
2  img = imread('lego_23_c500.png');
3
4  % Objects segmentation in 4 steps:
5  img_g = im2gray(img); % 1) convert from color to grayscale
6  % 2) Gaussian sigma=2 to smooth background and internal object's details
7  img_g_g = imgaussfilt(img_g,2);
8  % 3) Global auto-threshold and 4) invert output
9  img_g_g_bw = ~imbinarize(img_g_g,'global');
10
11 % Compute features of scalar type (also Centroid to show labels in image)
12 f_t = regionprops("table",img_g_g_bw,"Centroid",...
13  "Area","Circularity","ConvexArea","Eccentricity","EquivDiameter",...
14  "EulerNumber","Extent","FilledArea","MajorAxisLength",...
15  "MinorAxisLength","Orientation","Perimeter","Solidity");
16
17 t = tiledlayout(2,2);
18 nexttile, imshow(img), title('Original')
19 nexttile, imshow(img_g), title('Grayscale')
20 nexttile, imshow(img_g_g), title('Smoothed')
21 nexttile, imshow(img_g_g_bw), title('Segmented')
22 % Show the label (number) of the object on the image
23 hold on
24 for n=1:size(f_t,1) % n is the nth object
25     text(f_t.Centroid(n,1),f_t.Centroid(n,2),num2str(n),'Color','red')
26 end
27 hold off
28
29 imwrite(img_g_g_bw,'lego_23_c500_bw.png') % save segmented bw image
```

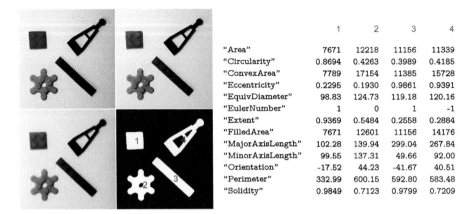

	1	2	3	4
"Area"	7671	12218	11156	11339
"Circularity"	0.8694	0.4263	0.3989	0.4185
"ConvexArea"	7789	17154	11385	15728
"Eccentricity"	0.2295	0.1930	0.9861	0.9391
"EquivDiameter"	98.83	124.73	119.18	120.16
"EulerNumber"	1	0	1	-1
"Extent"	0.9369	0.5484	0.2558	0.2884
"FilledArea"	7671	12601	11156	14176
"MajorAxisLength"	102.28	139.94	299.04	267.84
"MinorAxisLength"	99.55	137.31	49.66	92.00
"Orientation"	-17.52	44.23	-41.67	40.51
"Perimeter"	332.99	600.15	592.80	583.48
"Solidity"	0.9849	0.7123	0.9799	0.7209

FIGURE 25.2
Segmentation and computation of *scalar* type features using `regionprops` function. Images from left to right, top to bottom: original color image, grayscale image, smoothed image, and the result of the segmentation with the labels 1 to 4 of each connected component (object). On the right: the list of features and their corresponding values for each object.

2: Features of *coordinate* type

In this group of features, we highlight those features that output the co-ordinates (x, y), i.e., (`col`, `row`) of relevant properties of each connected component in the image.

- `"BoundingBox"`: smallest box that encloses the region. Outputs a vec-tor [`xmin ymin width height`], where `xmin ymin` are the x and y coordinates of the top left corner, and `width height` are the lengths of the box along x-axis and y-axis.

- `"Centroid"`: center of mass of the region. Outputs a vector [`x y`], where `x y` are the x and y coordinates of the centroid.

- `"ConvexHull"`: smallest convex polygon that encloses the region. Outputs a $n \times 2$ matrix V, where n is the number of vertices of the polygon. `V(n,1) V(n,2)` are the x and y coordinates of the nth vertex.

- `"Extrema"`: a set of coordinates indicating the extrema of the region. Outputs a 8×2 matrix E, where 8 is the number of possible extrema (some points may be the same). `E(e,1) E(e,2)` are the x and y coordinates of the eth extrema, organized as follows: $e = 1$ to 8 – top-left, top-right, right-top, right-bottom, bottom-right, bottom-left, left-bottom, left-top.

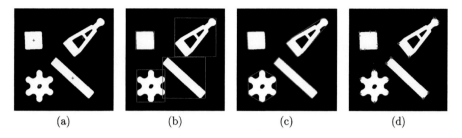

(a)   (b)   (c)   (d)

FIGURE 25.3
Features of *coordinate* type computed with `regionprops` function. (a) `"Centroid"`;
(b) `"BoundingBox"`; (c) `"ConvexHull"`; (d) `"Extrema"`.

In Listing 25.3 we compute the above features for image `lego_23_c500_bw.png`, created in Listing 25.2. Figure 25.3 presents the results superimposed on the input image.

LISTING 25.3
Computing features of *coordinate* type with `regionprops` function.

```
% Function regionprops, features of coordinate type
img = imread('lego_23_c500_bw.png');

% Compute features of coordinate type
f_t = regionprops("table",img,"Centroid",...
"BoundingBox","ConvexHull","Extrema");

tiledlayout(2,2)
ax1 = nexttile; imshow(img), title('Centroid')
ax2 = nexttile; imshow(img), title('BoundingBox')
ax3 = nexttile; imshow(img), title('ConvexHull')
ax4 = nexttile; imshow(img), title('Extrema')
% Show Centroid, BoundingBox, ConvexHull, Extrema
hold(ax1,'on'), hold(ax2,'on'), hold(ax3,'on'), hold(ax4,'on')
for n=1:size(f_t,1) % n is the nth object
    plot(ax1,f_t.Centroid(n,1),f_t.Centroid(n,2),...
        'r+','LineWidth',1)
    rectangle(ax2,'Position',f_t.BoundingBox(n,:),...
        'EdgeColor','r','LineWidth',1);
    line(ax3,f_t.ConvexHull{n}(:,1),f_t.ConvexHull{n}(:,2),...
        'Color','r','LineWidth',1);
    plot(ax4,f_t.Extrema{n}(:,1),f_t.Extrema{n}(:,2),...
        'r+','LineWidth',1)
end
hold(ax1,'off'), hold(ax2,'off'), hold(ax3,'off'), hold(ax4,'off')
```

3: Features of *image* type

In this group of features, we present those features that output an image based on the properties of each connected component.

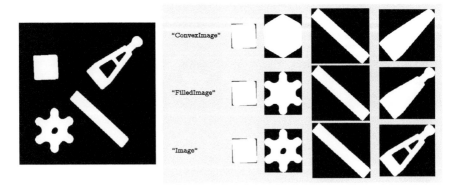

FIGURE 25.4
Features of *image* type computed with `regionprops` function. Left: input image. Right: each row shows an *image* type feature of the objects in the input image.

- "`ConvexImage`": smallest convex polygon that encloses the region. Outputs a binary image of the same size as the region's bounding box.
- "`FilledImage`": the original region without eventual internal holes. Outputs a binary image of the same size as the region's bounding box.
- "`Image`": the original region itself. Outputs a binary image of the same size as the region's bounding box.

In Listing 25.4 we compute the above features for image `lego_23_c500 _bw.png`, created on Listing 25.2. Figure 25.4 presents the results.

LISTING 25.4
Computing features of *image* type with `regionprops` function.

```
1  % Function regionprops, features of image type
2  img_bw = imread('lego_23_c500_bw.png');
3  figure, imshow(img_bw)
4
5  % Compute features of image type
6  f_i = regionprops("table",img_bw,"ConvexImage","FilledImage","Image");
7
8  % Show ConvexImage, FilledImage, Image
9  figure, t = tiledlayout(3,size(f_i,1));
10 t.TileSpacing = 'tight'; t.Padding = 'tight';
11 for n=1:size(f_i,1) % n is the nth object
12     nexttile, imshow(f_i.ConvexImage{n}),title(['ConvexImage ' num2str(n)])
13 end
14 for n=1:size(f_i,1) % n is the nth object
15     nexttile, imshow(f_i.FilledImage{n}),title(['FilledImage ' num2str(n)])
16 end
17 for n=1:size(f_i,1) % n is the nth object
18     nexttile, imshow(f_i.Image{n}),title(['Image ' num2str(n)])
19 end
```

4: Feret features

The maximum and minimum Feret diameters determine an object's largest and smallest widths.

- "MaxFeretProperties" returns:
  MaxFeretDiameter

  MaxFeretAngle

  MaxFeretCoordinates

- "MinFeretProperties" returns:
  MinFeretDiameter

  MinFeretAngle

  MinFeretCoordinates

These properties contain the following fields:

- *Diameter*: scalar representing the size of the line segment.
- *Angle*: in degrees, between the horizontal axis (0°) and the *Diameter* line segment. A positive angle is clockwise, and a negative is counterclockwise.
- *Coordinates*: of the endpoints of the *Diameter* line segment, in the form of a 2×2 matrix, where each row contains the x and y coordinates of an endpoint.

In Listing 25.5 we compute the above features for image lego_23_c500_bw.png, created on Listing 25.2. Figure 25.5 presents the results superimposed on the input image.

LISTING 25.5
Computing Feret features with regionprops function.

```
% Function regionprops, Feret features
img = imread('lego_23_c500_bw.png');

% Compute Feret features
f_t = regionprops("table",img,...
    "MaxFeretProperties","MinFeretProperties");

figure, imshow(img), title('MaxFeretProperties'), ax1 = gca;
figure, imshow(img), title('MinFeretProperties'), ax2 = gca;
% Show MaxFeretProperties, MinFeretProperties
hold(ax1,'on'), hold(ax2,'on')
for n=1:size(f_t,1) % n is the nth object
    imdistline(ax1,f_t.MaxFeretCoordinates{n}(:,1),...
        f_t.MaxFeretCoordinates{n}(:,2));
    angle_pos_max = mean(f_t.MaxFeretCoordinates{n})+20;
    text(ax1,angle_pos_max(1),angle_pos_max(2),...
        [num2str(round(f_t.MaxFeretAngle(n))) '^{\circ}'],'Color','red')
    imdistline(ax2,f_t.MinFeretCoordinates{n}(:,1),...
```

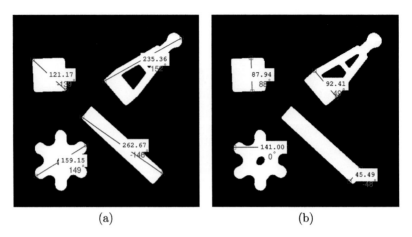

(a)   (b)

FIGURE 25.5
Feret features computed with `regionprops` function. Values in black are the *Diameter* and in red the *Angle*. (a) "MaxFeretFeatures"; (b) "MinFeretFeatures".

```
19        f_t.MinFeretCoordinates{n}(:,2));
20    angle_pos_min = mean(f_t.MinFeretCoordinates{n})+20;
21    text(ax2,angle_pos_min(1),angle_pos_min(2),...
22         [num2str(round(f_t.MinFeretAngle(n))) '^{\circ}'],'Color','red')
23 end
24 hold(ax1,'off'), hold(ax2,'off')
```

5: Features from grayscale pixel value

These features use the connected components (regions) as *masks* to operate on the pixels of the original (color or grayscale) image.

- "MaxIntensity": highest pixel value within the region.
- "MeanIntensity": mean value of all pixels within the region.
- "MinIntensity": lowest pixel value within the region.
- "PixelValues": the pixels within the region, encoded as a $p \times 1$ vector, where p is the number of pixels.
- "WeightedCentroid": center of region based on location and intensity value. Outputs a vector [x y], where x y are the x and y coordinates of the weighted centroid.

In Listing 25.6 we compute the above features for image `lego_23_c500 _bw.png`, created on Listing 25.2. Note that, besides the binary image, the grayscale is also an input parameter of `regionprops` function. Figure 25.6 presents the results.

	1	2	3	4
"MaxIntensity"	172	212	198	186
"MeanIntensity"	72.47	88.13	41.42	26.37
"MinIntensity"	26	1	0	0
"PixelValues"	7671x1 uint8	12218x1 uint8	11156x1 uint8	11339x1 uint8

FIGURE 25.6
Features from grayscale pixel value computed with `regionprops` function. From left to right: the boundaries of the binary regions are superimposed on the grayscale image; "Weighted-Centroid" feature; list of the other grayscale pixel value features and the corresponding values for each region.

LISTING 25.6
Computing features from grayscale pixel value with `regionprops` function.

```
% Function regionprops, features of grayscale pixel type
img = imread('lego_23_c500.png');
img_bw = imread('lego_23_c500_bw.png');
img_g = im2gray(img);
img_bw_b = boundarymask(img_bw);
img_g_r = imoverlay(img_g,img_bw_b);

% Compute features of grayscale pixel type
f_t = regionprops("table",img_bw,img_g,...
    "MaxIntensity","MeanIntensity","MinIntensity",...
    "PixelValues","WeightedCentroid");

tiledlayout(1,2)
nexttile; imshow(img_g_r), title('Grayscale pixels')
nexttile; imshow(img_bw), title('WeightedCentroid')
% Show WeightedCentroid
hold on
for n=1:size(f_t,1) % n is the nth object
    plot(f_t.WeightedCentroid(n,1),f_t.WeightedCentroid(n,2),...
        'r+','LineWidth',1)
    text(f_t.WeightedCentroid(n,1)+10,...
        f_t.WeightedCentroid(n,2)+10,num2str(n),'Color','red')
end
hold off
```

Discussion (Recipe notes)

In this recipe, you learned how to extract and visualize several region-based features from connected components into an image.

To access the connected components, besides the features of image type presented here, you can also use "`PixelIdxList`" (see Recipe 23), "`PixelList`", and "`SubarrayIdx`".

Most of our example code in this recipe uses MATLAB's `table` class (data type) to store the features, but you can also use an array of structures according to your preference, as we did in line 21 of Listing 25.1.

Features of *scalar* type can also be extracted and visualized interactively using the *Image Region Analyzer* App.

In the *Learn more about it* section you can find additional useful resources to deal with connected components, including the `bwpropfilt` function to facilitate the extraction of objects based on its features, and the `bwboundaries` and `bwtraceboundary` functions, which trace the boundaries of the objects.

Learn more about it

Useful MATLAB functions

Type the function name in the search field at www.mathworks.com/help/matlab/

· `compactitem` · `bwboundaries` · `bwconncomp` · `bwconvhull` · `bweuler` · `bwferet` · `bwperim` · `bwpropfilt` · `bwselect` · `bwtraceboundary` · `grayconnected` · `imdistline` · `line` · `rectangle` · `roipoly` · `roicolor` · `table` · `text` ·

MATLAB documentation, demos, and examples

- Classify Pixels That Are Partially Enclosed by ROI
  www.mathworks.com/help/images/classify-pixels-that-are-partially-enclosed-by-roi.html
- Create ROI Shapes
  www.mathworks.com/help/images/roi-creation-overview.html
- Detect and Measure Circular Objects in an Image
  www.mathworks.com/help/images/detect-and-measure-circular-objects-in-an-image.html
- Identifying Round Objects
  www.mathworks.com/help/images/identifying-round-objects.html
- Image Region Analyzer
  www.mathworks.com/help/images/ref/imageregionanalyzer-app.html
- Measuring Regions in Grayscale Images
  www.mathworks.com/help/images/measuring-regions-in-grayscale-images.html
- Region and Image Properties
  www.mathworks.com/help/images/pixel-values-and-image-statistics.html

Other sources

- Feret Diameter: Introduction
  https://blogs.mathworks.com/steve/2017/09/29/feret-diameter-introduction/

- Feret Properties – Wrapping Up
  https://blogs.mathworks.com/steve/2018/04/17/feret-properties-wrapping-up/

- Visualizing `regionprops` Ellipse Measurements
  https://blogs.mathworks.com/steve/2010/07/30/visualizing-regionprops-ellipse-measurements/

Notes

1 We used the *Local Graph Cut* method with a rectangular region of interest (ROI) that embraces the three objects, and *Subregion Density* parameter at maximum (slider at the rightest position). Except for some imperfections in the contours, especially for the toy ball, which is particularly difficult to segment due to many visual details, the results are quite good.
2 The `table` format is particularly recommended for visualization in the MATLAB Command Window.
3 See Section 3. Features of *image* type.
4 See also the `MaxFeretDiameter` field in "MaxFeretProperties".
5 See also the `MinFeretDiameter` field in "MinFeretProperties".
6 See also the `MaxFeretAngle` field in "MaxFeretProperties".
7 See Section 2. Features of *coordinate* type.

Part VIII

Color image processing

Part VIII – Color image processing

This Part is dedicated to some aspects of image processing that are *specific* to color images, such as the different ways by which color image contents can be encoded, as well as the differences between full-color image processing and pseudocolor image processing – and the practical usefulness of the latter.

Recipe 26 demonstrates the main characteristics of the color spaces available in MATLAB and teaches you how to perform conversions among them.

Recipe 27 shows how to adjust color images to make them more interpretable or visually pleasant, using different color spaces.

Recipe 28 teaches you how and when to use pseudocolor image processing techniques.

DOI: 10.1201/9781003170198-33

26

Recipe 26: Converting among different color spaces

This recipe teaches the main characteristics of the color spaces available in MATLAB and how to perform conversions among them.

Color perception is a psychophysiological experience that only occurs in systems equipped with sensors capable of differentiating wavelengths in the visible spectrum. In terms of human vision, these sensors are the *cone* photoreceptors found in the retina.

There are three types of cone cells, with peaks of responsiveness in the L (long), M (medium), and S (short) wavelengths, corresponding to what we call *primary colors of light*, i.e., red, green, and blue, respectively.

A large study with subjects concluded in 1931 was conducted by the CIE (*Commission Internationale de l'Eclairage*) [2] to obtain the amount of L, M, and S wavelengths required to be perceived as particular color by human observers. That study was the basis for creating the *CIE XYZ* (also known as CIE 1931) color space.

Manufacturers of color image acquisition equipment (like cameras and scanners) and reproduction devices (such as displays and printers) utilize a standardized conversion from the CIE XYZ color space to sRGB. This standardization facilitates dealing with the familiar *R, G, and B* components in both hardware and software settings. "Several standard image formats, including JPEG and PNG are based on sRGB color data, which makes sRGB the *de facto* standard for digital still cameras, color printers, and other imaging devices at the customer level [...] Thus, in practice, working with any RGB color data almost always means dealing with sRGB [10]."

In addition to CIE XYZ and RGB, several other color spaces have been designed to be more convenient and efficient for various applications. This recipe introduces different color spaces and their conversions, supported by MATLAB and its Image Processing Toolbox (IPT).

DOI: 10.1201/9781003170198-34

You will need (Ingredients)

- MATLAB R2020b or later
- MATLAB Image Processing Toolbox (IPT) version R2020b or later
- Image files: `allColors32k.png`, `fabric_pp_09.png`

Steps (Preparation)

1. Load an image file, a multidimensional array with the image in a specific color space, or create synthetic images directly specifying the pixels' values in the desired color space.

2. Check Figure 26.1 to see if a MATLAB function for direct conversion is available. Otherwise, use an intermediate conversion between the input and the desired output color space.

3. Apply the conversion using the selected *dedicated functions* or *color transformation structures*.

4. (OPTIONAL) Inspect the numerical values of the converted pixels and display the individual color channels in the form of intensity images[1].

Figure 26.1 presents the color spaces and conversions supported by MATLAB and the IPT. Conversions can be performed with either a *dedicated function* or a *color transformation structure*. A dedicated function follows the name format `in2out`, where `in` is the input (original) color space, and `out` is the output (converted) color space. A color transformation structure can be used to store the parameters for color conversion. Color transformation structures are created with the `makecform` function and applied with the `applycform` function. The main syntax of `makecform` requires the type of conversion specified by character vectors following the same name format `'in2out'` of a dedicated function.

Most conversions are obtained exclusively with either dedicated functions or color transformation structures. The following conversions can be done using both types of methods, but dedicated functions are preferred: instead of `'lab2srgb'` and `'srgb2lab'`, you should prefer `lab2rgb` and `rgb2lab`; instead of `'xyz2srgb'` and `'srgb2xyz'`, you should prefer `xyz2rgb` and `rgb2xyz`; instead of `'lab2xyz'` and `'xyz2lab'`, you should prefer `lab2xyz` and `xyz2lab`.

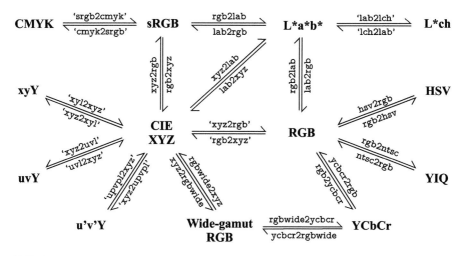

FIGURE 26.1
Color spaces and conversions supported by MATLAB's IPT. in2out is the name of a conversion-dedicated function. 'in2out' (with single quotes) is the character vector that identifies the conversion, to be used as an input parameter of makecform function.

The color spaces in Figure 26.1 are briefly explained next.

1: CIE XYZ and CIE chromaticity diagrams colors spaces

The CIE XYZ color space was designed to map the relationship between the physical wavelengths of visible light to the corresponding perceived colors by the human visual system. The traditional horseshoe-shaped CIE chromaticity diagrams, which aim to present all visible colors, are directly derived from CIE XYZ.

- **CIE XYZ** (xyz): Also known as CIE 1931 or XYZ. Y represents the luminance (achromatic information). CIE XYZ was obtained from an extensive experiment with volunteers to standardize the color perception of an average human observer. CIE XYZ is considered the root of all *tristimulus* color spaces.

- **xyY** (xyl): Results from a procedure that normalizes the XYZ values in order to describe the chromaticity of color in terms of x and y. $x = X/(X + Y + Z)$; $y = Y/(X + Y + Z)$; Y is the luminance of the CIE XYZ color space. Typically used to obtain the well-known *CIE x,y chromaticity diagram*, presenting all "pure" visible colors, i.e., with no luminance information.

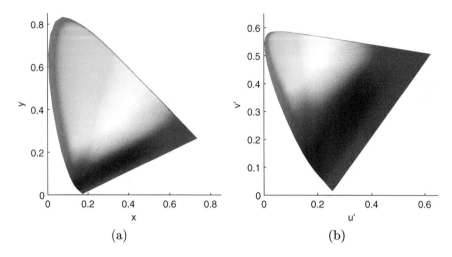

FIGURE 26.2
Chromaticity diagrams obtained with `plotChromaticity` function, presenting the visible spectrum inside the horseshoe-shaped contour. (a) CIE x,y chromaticity diagram. (b) CIE u′,v′ chromaticity diagram.

- **uvY²** (`uvl`): The u and v components, also known as CIE 1960 u and v, aim to deliver a more perceptually uniform[3] chromaticity diagram than the one obtained with x and y [22]. Y is the luminance of the CIE XYZ color space.
- **u′v′Y²** (`upvpl`): The u' and v' components, also known as CIE 1976 u' and v', are related to u and v as $u' = u$ and $v' = 1.5v$ [22, 13], and provide an improved chromaticity diagram in terms of perceptual uniformity, if compared to that obtained with u and v [20]. Y is the luminance of the CIE XYZ color space.

The `plotChromaticity` function generates CIE chromaticity diagrams. For a diagram based on x and y components, use `plotChromaticity` (no input is required); and for a diagram based on u′ and v′ components, use `plotChromaticity("ColorSpace","uv")`. Results are shown in Figure 26.2.

2: RGB color spaces

RGB color spaces are primarily designed for hardware-oriented purposes, serving as the internal color representation used by electronic devices such as monitors and displays. It may not be intuitive for users to specify colors in the RGB space.

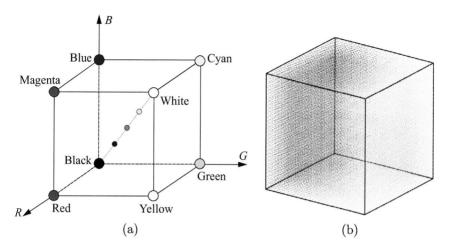

FIGURE 26.3
(a) The RGB cube and the locations of the primary colors, secondary colors, black, white, and gray levels. (b) Color cloud into the RGB color space of a synthetic image containing 32,768 equally spaced colors.

- **RGB** (rgb): Represented by a cube with red (*R*), green (*G*), and blue (*B*) axes. Figure 26.3(a) shows the RGB cube and the locations of the primary (red, green, blue) colors, secondary colors (mixture of two primaries at a time), black, white, and gray levels. The gray levels lie on the main diagonal of the cube, i.e., they are encoded with equal values of *R*, *G*, and *B*. Figure 26.3(b) shows the distribution of 32,768 equally spaced colors from the synthetic image allColors32k.png, in the RGB color cube, using a color cloud. To reproduce the Figure, load the image into a variable, for instance, img, and ask for the color cloud using colorcloud(img,'rgb').

- **sRGB** (srgb): Standard RGB. sRGB has become the widely accepted standard for various imaging devices, such as digital still cameras and displays, as evidenced by its adoption in popular image formats like JPEG and PNG. Consequently, handling RGB color data generated by most devices means we are working with sRGB [10].

- **Wide-gamut RGB** (rgbwide): the *color gamut* of a display represents the full range of colors it can accurately reproduce. Advancements in display technology aim to expand this gamut, among other improvements [8]. Color spaces such as wide-gamut RGB are designed to meet this growing demand.

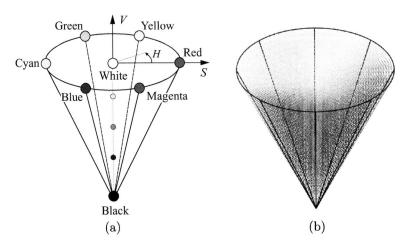

FIGURE 26.4
(a) The HSV inverted cone and the locations of the primary colors, secondary colors, black, white, and gray levels. (b) Color cloud into the HSV color space of a synthetic image containing 32,768 equally spaced colors.

3: Hue-oriented color spaces

In contrast to hardware-oriented color spaces, hue-oriented ones are primarily designed for intuitive specification and selection of colors. MATLAB adopts the HSV (hue, saturation, value) color space[4].

- **HSV** (`hsv`): Represented by an inverted cone, where each dimension is an intuitive attribute of color. Figure 26.4(a) shows the HSV inverted cone and the locations of the primary colors, secondary colors, black, white, and gray levels[5].
    Hue (H) – represents the "type" of color, often associated with the concept of "basic color" such as blue, red, or yellow. Related to the physical quantity *dominant wavelength*. In the HSV inverted cone, the H dimension is the angle.
    Saturation (S) – this characteristic is linked to the "purity" or "vividness" of a color. Higher saturation means greater purity and vividness while reducing saturation creates the impression of diluting the color with white. In the HSV inverted cone, the S dimension is the distance from the center to the edge (horizontal distance from the V axis).
    Value (V) – the achromatic component of the color. Related to the perceptual quantity *brightness*. In the HSV inverted cone, V is the height. A V value of 0 represents black, regardless of H and S. If S is set to 0, ranging V from 0 to 100%, we have gray levels, no matter the H. Figure 26.4(b) shows the distribution of 32,768 equally spaced colors

from the synthetic image `allColors32k.png`, in the HSV inverted cone, using a color cloud.

In Listing 26.1, we generate the primary and secondary colors of light, as well as black and white, in RGB coordinates and perform a conversion to HSV. Primary and secondary colors follow the sequence defined by the HSV inverted cone in Figure 26.4, as the H angle increases from 0°: Red, Yellow, Green, Cyan, Blue, Magenta.

LISTING 26.1
Converting from RGB to HSV color space.

```
1  % RGB to HSV color space conversion
2  % Specify in RGB: Black, Red, Yellow, Green, Cyan, Blue, Magenta, White
3  %      K  R  Y  G  C  B  M  W
4  r = [0  1  1  0  0  0  1  1];
5  g = [0  0  1  1  1  0  0  1];
6  b = [0  0  0  0  1  1  1  1];
7
8  img_rgb = cat(3, r, g, b); % 1x8 image with the specified colors
9  imshow(img_rgb,'InitialMagnification','fit');
10
11 img_hsv = rgb2hsv(img_rgb); % convert image from RGB to HSV
12
13 % Build a table to inspect colors' values in RGB and HSV
14 values = [reshape(img_rgb,[],3) reshape(img_hsv,[],3)];
15 T = array2table(values);
16 T.Properties.VariableNames = {'R','G','B','H','S','V'};
17 T.Properties.RowNames = {'Black','Red','Yellow','Green',...
18     'Cyan','Blue','Magenta','White'};
19 disp(T)
```

The resulting table T is presented next. In MATLAB, H, S, and V are represented with normalized values (range 0 to 1). Thus, the values for H are Red=0, Yellow=$\frac{1}{6}$=0.167, Green=$\frac{2}{6}$=0.333, Cyan=$\frac{3}{6}$=0.5, Blue=$\frac{4}{6}$=0.667, Magenta=$\frac{5}{6}$=0.833. Since the primary and secondary colors are positioned at the edge of the top (the "lid"[6]) of the inverted cone, S and V are equal to 1.

	R	G	B	H	S	V
Black	0	0	0	0	0	0
Red	1	0	0	0	1	1
Yellow	1	1	0	0.16667	1	1
Green	0	1	0	0.33333	1	1
Cyan	0	1	1	0.5	1	1
Blue	0	0	1	0.66667	1	1
Magenta	1	0	1	0.83333	1	1
White	1	1	1	0	0	1

To exemplify color specifications in HSV, we will obtain an orange, a pink, and a brown tone, derived from their intuitive descriptions:

FIGURE 26.5
Color specification in HSV. Orange: $H = \frac{1}{12}$, $S = 1$, $V = 1$; pink: $H = 0$, $S = 0.5$, $V = 1$;
brown: $H = \frac{1}{12}$, $S = 1$, $V = 0.5$.

Orange can be described as located *between red and yellow*. Given that
$H = 0$ is red and $H = \frac{1}{6}$ is yellow, $H = \frac{1}{12}$, with 100% of S and V
($S = 1$, $V = 1$) produce a tone of orange.

Pink can be described as a *whitish red*. Given that reducing saturation
creates the impression of diluting the color with white, a red ($H = 0$)
with S of 50% ($S = 0.5$) and value of 100% ($V = 1$) produces a tone of
pink.

Brown can be described as a *dark orange*. Given that the V dimension
represents the achromatic component of the color, an orange ($H = \frac{1}{12}$,
$S = 1$) with 50% of V ($V = 0.5$) produces a tone of brown.

Listing 26.2 implements these specified tones of orange, pink, and brown.
An HSV to RGB conversion is applied since `imshow` requires images in RGB.
Figure 26.5 shows the result.

LISTING 26.2
Specifying colors in HSV.

```
1  % Color specification in HSV
2  % Specify in HSV: Orange, Pink, Brown
3  %       O      P      Br
4  h = [1/12     0    1/12];
5  s = [ 1      0.5    1 ];
6  v = [ 1       1    0.5];
7
8  img_hsv = cat(3, h, s, v); % 1x3 image with the specified colors
9  img_rgb = hsv2rgb(img_hsv); % convert from HSV to RGB
10 imshow(img_rgb,'InitialMagnification','fit');
```

4: Perceptually uniform color spaces

Perceptually uniform color spaces are designed to reproduce the human
perception of differences between colors. Thus, equal distances in the color
space are reasonable approximations of equal perceived differences in color
appearance.

- **L*a*b*** (`lab`): Also known as CIE LAB or CIE 1976 L*a*b*. L* represents the luminance (achromatic), a* represents the magenta-green,
  and b* represents the yellow-blue content of color. Gray levels are
  represented by a*=b*=0 and L* ranging from 0 (black) to 100 (white).

Positive values of a* represent magenta tones, while negative values of a* represent green tones. Positive values of b* represent yellow tones, while negative values of b* represent blue tones. a* and b* are not explicitly constrained and typically assume values from -128 to 127. The distance between colors $C1$ and $C2$ in L*a*b* is computed as $\Delta E_{ab}^* = [(L_{c1}^* - L_{c2}^*)^2 + (a_{c1}^* - b_{c2}^*)^2 + (b_{c1}^* - b_{c2}^*)^2]^{1/2}$, and is available in MATLAB's IPT `deltaE` function.

We can use Listing 26.1 as a template to convert primary colors, secondary colors, black and white, from RGB to L*a*b*. All that is needed is to change the function in line 11 to `rgb2lab`, and change the names of the rows in `T.Properties.RowNames`, and rename all necessary variables accordingly.

The resulting table `T` is presented next. Since a* represents magenta(positive)-green(negative), the larger positive value in this example occurs at Magenta (98.234), and the larger negative value at Green (-86.183). Similarly, since b* represents yellow(positive)-blue(negative), the larger positive value in this example occurs at Yellow (94.478), and the larger negative value at Blue (-107.86).

	R	G	B	L*	a*	b*
Black	0	0	0	0	0	0
Red	1	0	0	53.241	80.092	67.203
Yellow	1	1	0	97.139	-21.554	94.478
Green	0	1	0	87.735	-86.183	83.179
Cyan	0	1	1	91.113	-48.088	-14.131
Blue	0	0	1	32.297	79.188	-107.86
Magenta	1	0	1	60.324	98.234	-60.825
White	1	1	1	100	0	0

- **L*ch** (`lch`): Also know as LCH or L*C*h$_{ab}$. It is derived from the L*a*b* color space, obtained by means of a rectangular to polar transformation on a* and b* values. The h dimension represents the hue, and c is called chroma. L*ch is used in the CIE 1994 color difference metric [22], available in MATLAB's IPT `imcolordiff` function. L*ch also finds applications, for example, in the design of color palettes for statistical data visualization [25, 24].

5: TV and video color spaces

The TV and video color spaces discussed here are based on two key principles rooted in historical reasons. Firstly, they decouple luminance from chromaticity, enabling compatibility with older black-and-white systems. Secondly, these spaces represent colors by utilizing color differences rather than their absolute values, which in turn reduces the bandwidth required for signal transmission.

- **YIQ** (`ntsc`): The Y component represents the luminance (achromatic), while I and Q components encode the color information, based on color differences. I stands for *in-phase* and Q stands for *quadrature*. These terms are related to the modulation scheme employed in the transmission of analog TV signals, as specified by the National Television System Committee (NTSC) standard. In YIQ color space, Y is derived from the RGB components using the equation $Y = 0.2989R + 0.5870G + 0.1140B$. Y can range from 0 (black) to 1 (white) and is commonly regarded as the grayscale representation of an RGB image. In MATLAB, this RGB to grayscale conversion is available with the `rgb2gray` function[7].

Another possible method to convert an image from RGB to grayscale is averaging the *R, G, and B* components. However, it's not always the most accurate representation of perceived luminance due to the way human vision works.

The human visual system does not perceive the three colors (red, green, and blue) with equal sensitivity. Green is perceived as being the brightest, followed by red and then blue. As a result, a more common formula for converting RGB to grayscale that considers human perception is: `Grayscale=0.299×R+0.587×G+0.114×B`. This weighted sum gives more prominence to the green channel, reflecting its higher perceived brightness.

So, while averaging is acceptable and will give you a grayscale image, the weighted sum approach is often preferred for a more perceptually accurate result. This becomes particularly visible if we use saturated colors to compare both conversion methods, as Listing 26.3 exemplifies. Results are shown in Figure 26.6, where the bar's saturated red, green, and blue in part (b) become indistinguishable for the average method.

LISTING 26.3
Converting from RGB to grayscale using two different approaches.

```
 1 % RGB to grayscale conversion using two methods
 2 b = bar(1:3,'FaceColor','flat'); % an arbitrary bar plot with 3 bars
 3 xticks([]), yticks([])
 4 % [R G B] values specifying 1st,2nd,3rd bars colors as red,green,blue
 5 b.CData(1,:) = [1 0 0]; b.CData(2,:) = [0 1 0]; b.CData(3,:) = [0 0 1];
 6 % Store the plot as a raster image using the screen resolution
 7 img = print('-RGBImage','-r0');
 8
 9 % Method 1: grayscale = (R+G+B)/3
10 img_gray_1 = imlincomb(1/3,img(:,:,1),1/3,img(:,:,2),1/3,img(:,:,3));
11 % Method 2: grayscale = Y = 0.2989*R + 0.5870*G + 0.1140*B
12 img_gray_2 = rgb2gray(img);
13
14 figure, imshowpair (img_gray_1, img_gray_2, 'montage')
```

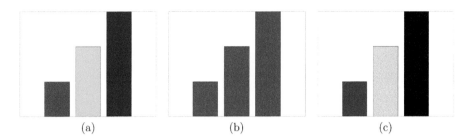

FIGURE 26.6
RGB to grayscale convertion. (a) Original image. (b) Converted image using the average of *R, G, and B*. (c) Converted image using rgb2gray function.

- **YCbCr** (ycbcr): The Y component represents the luminance (achromatic), while Cb and Cr components encode the color information as differences between blue and a reference value, and red and a reference value. YCbCr is adopted in image compression (e.g., JPEG) and digital video (e.g., H.264) standards.

  Beware that the Y component resulting from an RGB to YCbCr conversion (rgb2ycbcr function) does not occupy the full range[8] of the image's class (data type) and, therefore, it is *not* an adequate grayscale representation of an RGB image, such as the Y component in the YIQ model.

6: Printing color spaces

The above color models in this recipe are based on the *additive mixture of lights*. In contrast, a printing color space is based on the *additive mixture of pigments*, also called *subtractive mixture of lights*. A primary color of pigment absorbs a primary color of light and reflects the other two. Thus, cyan (absorbs red, reflects blue and green), magenta (absorbs green, reflects red and blue), and yellow (absorbs blue, reflects red and green) are commonly adopted as the primary colors of pigments for use in color printing devices.

- **CMYK** (cmyk): C, M, and Y stand for the primaries cyan, magenta, and yellow. In practice, the mixture of these three pigments results in a faded black, so the K (black) pigment is added as a fourth component of the color space. In its simplest form, the primaries C, M, Y, and K can be obtained from $R, G, and B$ (in the range 0...1) as $C = 1 - R$; $M = 1 - G$; $Y = 1 - B$; $K = min(C, M, Y)$.

Listing 26.4 shows a conversion from RGB to CMYK of an image of fabrics with colors predominantly cyan, magenta, yellow, and black. The conversion is performed with makecform and applycform functions. Line 9 makes a row-wise concatenation of the converted image's C, M, Y, and K components.

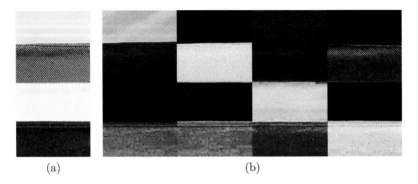

(a)   (b)

FIGURE 26.7
RGB to CMYK conversion: (a) is the original RGB image and (b) are the C, M, Y, and K components of the converted CMYK image, presented as intensity images. The largest C, M, Y, and K
values occur at the corresponding regions with predominant cyan, magenta, yellow, and black
colors in the original image.

Results are shown in Figure 26.7. Note that the predominant color appears
more intensely in its correspondent channel.

LISTING 26.4
Converting from RGB to CMYK color space.

```
% RGB to CMYK color space conversion
img = imread('fabric_pp_09.png');
img = rot90(img); % rotate image 90 deg counterclockwise
imshow(img), title('Original')

c = makecform('srgb2cmyk');   % c is a structure to specify...
img_cmyk = applycform(img,c); % ...the conversion

img_cmyk_2d = img_cmyk(:,:);   % MxNx4 to row-wise MxN*4
figure, imshow(img_cmyk_2d), title('C,M,Y,K components')
```

Discussion (Recipe notes)

In this recipe, you learned the main characteristics of several color spaces
and explored how to perform conversions among them, using either *dedicated
functions* (format in2out) or *color transformation structures* (makecform and
applycform functions).

   Color perception and color spaces are immensely vast topics, encompassing a myriad of aspects, from the physics of light to the intricacies of human
vision and data encoding, among others. You are encouraged to explore these
topics further, starting from the references in the *Learn more about it* section
below.

Learn more about it

Useful MATLAB functions

Type the function name in the search field at www.mathworks.com/help/
matlab/

· applycform · colorcloud · deltaE · hsv2rgb · im2gray
· imcolordiff · imlincomb · lab2rgb · lab2xyz · ntsc2rgb · rgb2hsv
· rgb2lab · rgb2ntsc · rgb2xyz · hsv2rgb · lab2rgb · lab2xyz
· measureColor · ntsc2rgb · plotChromaticity · rgb2gray · rgb2hsv
· rgb2lab · rgb2ntsc · rgb2xyz · lab2rgb · rgb2ycbcr · rgbwide2xyz
· · rgbwide2ycbcr · xyz2lab · xyz2rgb · xyz2rgbwide · ycbcr2rgb
· ycbcr2rgbwide ·

MATLAB documentation, demos, and examples

- Calculate CIE94 Color Difference of Colors on Test Chart
  www.mathworks.com/help/images/calculate-cie94-color-differences
  -of-colors-measured-on-test-chart.html

- Color Space Conversions, Support for International Color Consortium
  (ICC) Profiles
  www.mathworks.com/help/images/color.html

- Device-Independent Color Spaces
  www.mathworks.com/help/images/device-independent-color-spaces.
  html

- Implement Digital Camera Processing Pipeline
  www.mathworks.com/help/images/end-to-end-implementation-of-
  digital-camera-processing-pipeline.html

- Understanding Color Spaces and Color Space Conversion
  www.mathworks.com/help/images/understanding-color-spaces-and-
  color-space-conversion.html

Notes

1 Remember that `imshow` and similar functions expect an RGB image as input.
2 Do not mistake for the TV-oriented YUV color space [10], or for the perceptually
   uniform CIE LUV (also known as L*u*v*) color space. YUV and CIE LUV are not
   available in MATLAB's IPT.
3 Perceptually uniform color spaces will be discussed later in this recipe.
4 HSB (hue, saturation, brightness) is generally accepted to denote the same color
   space. There are variations of the HSV, such as HSI (hue, saturation, intensity)
   and HLS (hue, luminance, saturation). It is important to mention that different

interpretations of these acronyms can occur. Thus, it is important to verify the current set of equations employed to convert from RGB to one of these color spaces (see [5] for details).

5 To reproduce Figure 26.4(b), load the image into a variable, for instance, `img`, and ask for the color cloud using `colorcloud(img,'hsv')`.

6 The "lid" of the HSV inverted cone originates what is commonly called a *color wheel*.

7 Note that starting with R2020b, MATLAB also includes the `im2gray` function that spares the user from having to ensure that the image is indeed RGB before calling the `rgb2gray` function.

8 According to the documentation: "The range of numeric values depends on the data type of the image. YCbCr does not use the full range of the image data type so that the video stream can include additional (non-image) information."

27

Recipe 27: Color image adjustments

This recipe teaches you how to adjust color images to make them more interpretable or visually pleasant, using different color spaces.

Previously[1], we have used MATLAB to adjust the brightness, contrast, and overall appearance of grayscale images. Extending these operations to color images might lead to additional challenges and unexpected results, such as the appearance of spurious colors in the resulting image.

In this recipe, depending on the image processing operation, we adopt one of these strategies to ensure correct results:

1. Separate the achromatic (brightness) and chromatic (color) elements of the original image and:
   - Modify only the achromatic component while preserving the chromatic components.
   - Modify the chromatic components while monitoring the resulting output to prevent unwanted alterations in the perceived colors.
2. Apply the same adjustments to the red, green, and blue components of the RGB color space to ensure minimal changes in the perceived colors.

You will need (Ingredients)

- MATLAB R2019b or later
- MATLAB Image Processing Toolbox (IPT) version R2019b or later
- (OPTIONAL[2]) One or more of your images

Steps (Preparation)

1: Contrast improvement using histogram equalization

1. Load the image into the workspace.

DOI: 10.1201/9781003170198-35

2. Extract the luminance channel using the `rgb2lab` function.

3. Apply histogram equalization to the luminance channel.

4. Recover the adjusted image with the `lab2rgb` function.

5. Display *before* and *after* images and (visually) evaluate the quality of the results.

The code in Listing 27.1 performs the histogram equalization of the L* channel of the L*a*b* (CIELAB) color space using two methods – global histogram equalization with `histeq` function and local histogram equalization with `adapthisteq` function[3].

LISTING 27.1

Color histogram equalization.

```
1  % Color histogram equalization
2  img = imread('office_4.jpg');
3  lab = rgb2lab(img);
4  l = lab(:,:,1); % L* channel
5  l = l/100; % Values [0...100] of the L* -> [0...1]
6
7  l_g = histeq(l,256); % method (1) global histogram equalization
8  l_g = l_g*100; % Values [0...1] of the processed L* -> [0...100]
9  l_l = adapthisteq(l); % method (2) local histogram equalization
10 l_l = l_l*100; % Values [0...1] of the processed L* -> [0...100]
11
12 lab_g = cat(3, l_g, lab(:,:,2), lab(:,:,3));
13 lab_l = cat(3, l_l, lab(:,:,2), lab(:,:,3));
14 img_l_g = lab2rgb(lab_g);
15 img_l_l = lab2rgb(lab_l);
16 figure, montage({img, img_l_g, img_l_l})
17 title('in, L* global hist eq, L* local hist eq')
```

Comparing the results after global or local histogram equalization (Figure 27.1), we can note that both variations of the histogram equalization method improve the perceived contrast while preserving the original colors (hues). Upon closer inspection, we can see that the local histogram equalization results (Figure 27.1(c)) allow for better visualization of the originally dark objects at the left corner of the table while at the same time preserving the details on the monitor.

2: Saturation adjustment in the HSV color space

1. Load the image into the workspace.

2. Extract the saturation channel using the `rgb2hsv` function.

3. Apply a "boost" to the saturation channel.

4. Recover the adjusted image with the `hsv2rgb` function.

5. Display *before* and *after* images and (visually) evaluate the quality of the results.

(a)   (b)   (c)

FIGURE 27.1
Color histogram equalization. (a) Original image. (b) Processed image using global histogram equalization. (c) Processed image using local histogram equalization.

The code in Listing 27.2 modifies the saturation color channel using two distinct approaches – a *multiplicative gain* and an *additive offset*. To allow a comparison between the approaches, the constants `gain` and `offset` were chosen so that the percentage of pixels with *S* values larger than 1, after the respective operations, were approximately 3%.

LISTING 27.2
Modifying the saturation color channel: two different approaches.

```
% Color HSV S manipulation
img = imread ('peacock.jpg');
[n_r, n_c] = size(img, 1, 2);
n_t = n_r*n_c; % Total number of pixels

hsv = rgb2hsv(img);
s = hsv(:,:,2);

gain = 1.7;
offset = 0.4;

s_g = s*gain;    % Multiplicative gain
s_g_L = s_g > 1;
s_g_L_p = sum(s_g_L(:))/n_t % Proportion of pixels with S>1 after gain
s_o = s+offset; % Additive offset
s_o_L = s_o>1;
s_o_L_p = sum(s_o_L(:))/n_t % Proportion of pixels with S>1 after offset

hsv_s_g = cat(3, hsv(:,:,1), s_g, hsv(:,:,3));
hsv_s_o = cat(3, hsv(:,:,1), s_o, hsv(:,:,3));
img_s_g = hsv2rgb(hsv_s_g);
img_s_o = hsv2rgb(hsv_s_o);
figure, montage({img, img_s_g, img_s_o});
title('in, S*gain, S+offset')
```

Figure 27.2 shows the results. In both cases, as expected, as the saturation increases, image colors appear more vivid or vibrant[4].

(a)   (b)   (c)

FIGURE 27.2
HSV-based adjustments. (a) Original image. (b) Processed image using multiplicative gain of
`S*gain`. (c) Processed image using an additive offset of `S+offset`.

3: RGB-based adjustment

1. Load the image into the workspace.
2. Apply the same operations on the R, G, and B color channels.
3. Display *before* and *after* images and (visually) evaluate the quality of the results.

In Recipe 13, we performed gamma correction on RGB images, using the same value of γ for each color channel. We follow the same principle in Listing 27.3 where we apply a sigmoid function to the image's R, G, and B channels.

LISTING 27.3
Applying a sigmoid function to enhance contrast in RGB images.

```
% Color R, G, B sigmoid
img = imread('wagon.jpg');

x = 0:255; inflec = 127;
slope = 0.025;  % smoother slope
% slope = 0.05; % sharper slope
sigmoid = uint8(255./((1+exp(-slope*(x-inflec)))));
figure, plot(sigmoid); xlim([0 255]) ; ylim([0 255]) ; grid on

img_s = intlut(img, sigmoid);
figure, montage({img, img_s})
```

Figure 27.3 shows the results. The sigmoid maps pixel values below `inflec = 127` to lower values and values above `inflec = 127` to higher values. The higher the slope, the more vivid or vibrant the perceived output colors.

4: Low-light enhancement

1. Load the image into the workspace.

(a)   (b)   (c)

FIGURE 27.3
RGB-based adjustment. (a) Original image. (b) Processed image using a sigmoid function with `slope = 0.025`. (c) Processed image using a sigmoid function with a sharper slope (`slope = 0.05`).

2. Enhance the image using the `imlocalbrighten` function.
3. Display *before* and *after* images and (visually) evaluate the quality of the results.

Improving images captured in notably low-light conditions is challenging. While traditional methods aimed at enhancing brightness or contrast can improve visibility in darker areas, they often result in the oversaturation of the image's brighter regions.

The `imlocalbrighten` function implements a low-light image enhancement method that addresses this issue. It is based on an image dehazing technique and the empirical observation that the negative of an RGB low-light image approximates to a hazy image [11]. Internally, `imlocalbrighten` complements[5] the *R, G, and B* channels of the input image, applies the dehazing process, and then complements the *R, G, and B* channels again to produce the enhanced image.

Listing 27.4 presents a simple example, where the `amount` parameter (within the range [0...1]) is used to specify the intensity of the brightening operation. The default value is 1. Figure 27.4 shows results for `amount=0.1` and `amount=0.9`.

LISTING 27.4
Low-light enhancement.

```
% Color low-light enhancement
img = imread ('car_3.jpg');

amount = 0.1;
%amount = 0.9;
img_lle = imlocalbrighten(img, amount);
figure, montage({img, img_lle})
```

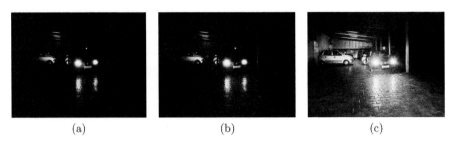

(a)   (b)   (c)

FIGURE 27.4
Low-light image enhancement. (a) Original image. (b) Processed image with amount=0.1. (c) Processed image with amount=0.9.

Discussion (Recipe notes)

In this recipe, you learned how to manipulate color images to enhance their overall visual appeal or emphasize specific details while preserving the perceived hue dimension of the colors, which is the attribute commonly associated with the "color name."

We strongly encourage exploring the resources in the *Learn more about it* section below for additional insights and examples.

Learn more about it

Useful MATLAB functions

Type the function name in the search field at www.mathworks.com/help/matlab/
· adapthisteq · histeq · hsv2rgb · imlocalbrighten · intlut · lab2rgb · rgb2hsv · rgb2lab ·

MATLAB documentation, demos, and examples

- Adjust the Contrast of Color
  www.mathworks.com/help/vision/ug/adjust-the-contrast-of-color-images.html
- Convert Between RGB and HSV Color Spaces
  www.mathworks.com/help/images/convert-from-hsv-to-rgb-color-space.html
- Low-Light Image Enhancement
  www.mathworks.com/help/images/low-light-image-enhancement.html

Notes

1   Parts III and IV of the book, particularly Recipes 8, 11, 12, and 13.
2   The recipe has been prepared using MATLAB's built-in images.
3   See Recipe 8.
4   Since the performed offset operation shifts the entire S dimension by a large constant (0.4 corresponds to 40% of the $[0...1]$ S range), the effect on the image in part (c) is more prominent if compared to the multiplicative gain in part (b).
5   Complementing an image is the same as computing its negative. See Recipe 11.

28

Recipe 28: Image pseudocoloring

This recipe teaches you how to apply pseudocoloring techniques to grayscale images.

Pseudocoloring is a technique in image processing where each gray level in an image is mapped to a specific color, enhancing the contrast and visualization of features in monochromatic images. Pseudocoloring is commonly used in medical imaging, remote sensing, and microscopy to enhance the visibility of specific features that might be indistinguishable in grayscale.

The main types of pseudocoloring techniques include density slicing, where distinct color ranges represent different intensity bands, and domain-specific colormaps, such as the "hot" and "cold" maps used in thermal imaging. By applying these techniques, interpreters can extract meaningful information from the data more readily than by examining the original grayscale image.

You will need (Ingredients)

- MATLAB R2020b or later
- MATLAB Image Processing Toolbox (IPT) version 2020b or later
- **Image:** AD21-0016-001_F3_P3_knife_plane_drop_v~orig.tif[1].

Steps (Preparation)

1. Load grayscale image.
2. Choose the desired colormap from the several MATLAB's pre-defined colormaps; alternatively, edit/create your own colormap.
3. (OPTIONAL) Use rgbplot function to view the R, G, and B components of the colormap.

DOI: 10.1201/9781003170198-36

4. If necessary, reduce the number of gray levels of the image to N, using the `grayslice` function, and set the number of colors in the colormap to N.

5. Apply the desired colormap to the grayscale image, usually as a parameter of `imshow` function.

6. Save the pseudocolored image providing the colormap as an input parameter for the function `imwrite`.

To apply pseudocolors to a grayscale image in MATLAB, we employ the *indexed image* representation, which links a specific *colormap* to the grayscale image[2].

MATLAB provides several pre-defined colormaps with different color combinations through specific functions following the colormaps' names. These functions receive the number of colors N as input and output the $N \times 3$ colormap[3]. Typing the command below, for example, you get the `flag` colormap, which cycles the red, white, blue, and black colors.

```
cm = flag(5)
```

```
cm =
      1       0       0
      1       1       1
      0       0       1
      0       0       0
      1       0       0
```

Listing 28.1 presents the pseudocoloring of a Schlieren photography of shock waves produced by a supersonic jet [14], using `pink`, `turbo`, and `hot` colormaps. Download the *original* image from NASA Image and Video Library[1]. To save the image, provide the desired colormap as an input parameter to the `imwrite` function (line 12). Figure 28.1 shows the results. Note that the version with the hot colormap approximates one of those in [14].

LISTING 28.1
Pseudocoloring with different colormaps.

```
1  % Grayscale image pseudocolored with "pink", "turbo" and "hot" colormaps
2  img = imread('AD21-0016-001_F3_P3_knife_plane_drop_v~orig.tif');
3  img = rot90(img,-1); % rotate image 90 deg clockwise
4
5  figure
6  t = tiledlayout(1,4);
7  nexttile, imshow(img), title('Original grayscale')
8  nexttile, imshow(img,pink), title('pink colormap')
9  nexttile, imshow(img,turbo), title('turbo colormap')
10 nexttile, imshow(img,hot),title('hot colormap')
11
12 imwrite(img,hot,'pseudocolored.png')
```

One of the main motivations to produce a pseudocolocor version of a grayscale image is to improve the visualization of details, since our ability to

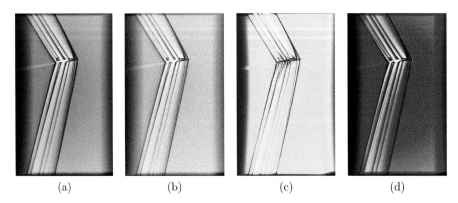

FIGURE 28.1
Grayscale image (a) pseudocolored with different colormaps: (b) `pink`; (c) `turbo`, and (d) `hot`.
Original image: courtesy of NASA.

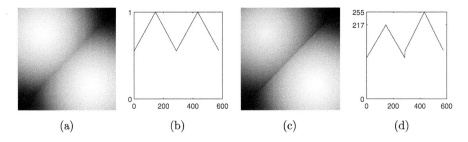

FIGURE 28.2
Synthetic grayscale image with two "elevations." In (a), the peaks are equal, as shown in the respective diagonal line profile across the peaks in (b). In (c), the left peak is 15% attenuated so that the maximum is at gray level 217, as shown in the respective diagonal line profile across the peaks in (d).

discriminate colors is much greater than our ability to discriminate shades of gray[4]. In Listing 28.2 we generate a synthetic image containing two grayscale "elevations" (function `bwdist`), and multiply the left one by 0.85 (15% attenuation). Figure 28.2 presents the images before and after the attenuation, accompanied by *line profile* plots (`improfile` function) showing the pixels' values of the diagonal across the peaks of the image. The image is then saved as `synthPeaks2_gray_uneven.png` to be pseudocolored.

LISTING 28.2
Generating a synthetic grayscale image to be pseudocolored.

```
1 % Generate synthetic grayscale image to further apply pseudocolors
2 img = zeros(407, 407); % a 407x407 image
3 img(103,103) = 1; img(307,307) = 1; % two nonzero pixels
4 % Distance transform: for every p, Euclid. dist. to nearest nonzero pixel
5 img_d = bwdist(img);
6 img_d_r = mat2gray(img_d); % rescale min->0, max->1
```

```
7  img_d_r_c = 1 - img_d_r; % complement (photographic negative)
8
9  % Atenuate 15% of left "elevation"
10 t = rot90(triu(ones(407,407)))*0.85;
11 t(~t) = 1;
12 img_d_r_c_a = img_d_r_c.*t;
13 img_d_r_c_a_u = im2uint8(img_d_r_c_a); % double [0...1] to uint8 [0...255]
14
15 % Show grayscale's equal and unequal peaks
16 figure
17 tiledlayout(1,4);
18 nexttile, imshow(img_d_r_c), title('Equal peaks')
19 nexttile, improfile(img_d_r_c,[1 407],[1 407]); title('Diag. profile')
20 ylim([0 1]), yticks([0 1]),
21 nexttile, imshow(img_d_r_c_a_u), title('Left peak 15% attenuation')
22 nexttile, improfile(img_d_r_c_a_u,[1 407],[1 407]); title('Diag. profile')
23 ylim([0 255]), yticks([0 217 255]),
24
25 imwrite(img_d_r_c_a_u,'synthPeaks2_gray_uneven.png')
```

The code in Listing 28.3 applies pseudocolors to the synthetic image created in Listing 28.2, using the `jet` colormap and 10 colors (stored in variable s on line 4). To reduce the number of gray levels of the original image, we use the `grayslice` function. It performs a *multilevel thresholding* with linearly spaced thresholds and remaps the image accordingly (line 5). If you use the `jet` colormap without specifying the value of s, you will get the results in Figure 28.3 (b) (with the default 256 colors). This pseudocoloring technique is commonly named as *intensity slicing*. Results are shown in Figure 28.3. Figure 28.3(c) presents a `colorbar` depicting the correspondence between the remapped values and the colors. As expected, the color of the lower peak is orange, indicating that it is in second from the last range due to the applied attenuation.

LISTING 28.3
Generating a synthetic grayscale image and applying pseudocolors.

```
1  % Pseudocoloring with 256 colors and "intensity slicing" with 10 partitions
2  img = imread('synthPeaks2_gray_uneven.png');
3
4  s = 10; % number of slices for the "intensity slicing"
5  img_s = grayslice(img, s); % multithreshold and remap
6
7  figure
8  tiledlayout(1,3);
9  nexttile, imshow(img), title('Grayscale')
10 nexttile, imshow(img, jet); title('Pseudoc. 256 colors')
11 nexttile, imshow(img_s, jet(s)); title('Pseudoc. s colors')
12 colorbar
13
14 imwrite(img_s,jet(s),'pseudocolored_slices.png')
```

In addition to using MATLAB's built-in colormaps, we can also create our own.

Listing 28.4 shows code to create a colormap ranging from black to white, with tones of cyan in between. The exponential mathematical functions (lines

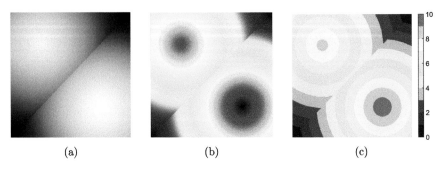

(a)   (b)   (c)

FIGURE 28.3

Pseudocoloring a synthetic grayscale image with two "elevations." (a) The grayscale image where the left peak is 15% attenuated. (b) Pseudocoloring with jet colormap, 256 colors. (c) Pseudocoloring with jet colormap and *intensity slicing* with 10 partitions.

4–6) ensure that each channel has values between 0 and 1. The code uses the rgbplot function to visualize the resulting R, G, and B components of the designed colormap. Figure 28.4 shows the results.

LISTING 28.4

Creating a customized colormap.

```
 1  % Pseudocoloring with a users' created colormap
 2  img = imread('synthPeaks2_gray_uneven.png');
 3
 4  r = linspace(0,1,256).^4;     % function for the R component of the colormap
 5  g = linspace(0,1,256).^0.35; % function for the G component of the colormap
 6  b = linspace(0,1,256).^0.3;  % function for the B component of the colormap
 7  cm = [r' g' b']; % assembly into colormap's format
 8
 9  s = 10; % number of slices for the "intensity slicing"
10  img_s = grayslice(img, s); % multithreshold and remap
11  idx = round(linspace(1,256,s)); % s equidistant indices to downsample cm
12  cm_s = cm(idx,:); % downsample cm from 256 to s colors
13
14  % Show R,G,B of the colormaps and the respective pseudocolored images
15  figure
16  tiledlayout(1,4);
17  nexttile, rgbplot(cm)
18  xlim([1 256]), title('R,G,B of the 256 colors colormap')
19  nexttile, imshow(img, cm), title('Pseudoc. 256 colors')
20  nexttile, rgbplot(cm_s)
21  xlim([1 s]), title('R,G,B of the 10 colors colormap')
22  nexttile, imshow(img_s, cm_s), title('Pseudoc. 10 colors')
23  colorbar
24
25  imwrite(img_s,cm_s,'pseudocolored_slices_custom_cm.png')
```

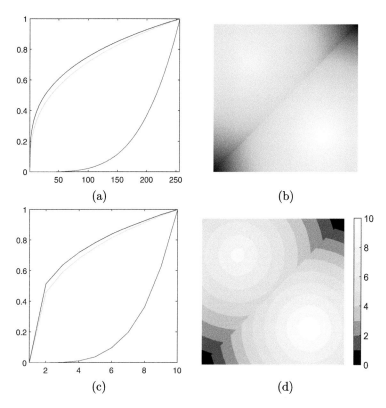

FIGURE 28.4

Customized colormap created using exponential functions. The plots are obtained with rgb-plot function, which shows the colormap's R, G, and B components. (a) is a colormap with 256 colors, and (c) with 10 colors. (b) and (d) are the respective pseudocolorized images.

Discussion (Recipe notes)

In this recipe, you learned how to apply pseudocolors to a grayscale image to improve its visualization. MATLAB provides several pre-defined colormaps, but you can also edit them or design your own colormaps.

We strongly encourage exploring the resources below for additional insights and examples.

Learn more about it

Useful MATLAB functions

Type the function name in the search field at `www.mathworks.com/help/matlab/`

· `bwdist` · `colorbar` · `colormap` · `grayslice` · `linspace` · `rgbplot` · `tiledlayout` ·

MATLAB documentation, demos, and examples

- Colormap Editor
  `www.mathworks.com/help/matlab/ref/colormapeditor.html`
- Colormaps
  `www.mathworks.com/help/images/convert-from-hsv-to-rgb-color-space.html`
- How Image Data Relates to a Colormap
  `www.mathworks.com/help/matlab/creating_plots/how-image-data-relates-to-a-colormap.html`

Notes

1 Available at: `https://images.nasa.gov/details/AD21-0016-001_F3_P3_knife_plane_drop_v`
2 In Recipe 10, you can find an inspection of an indexed image using the *Pixel Region* tool (Figure 10.1). Thus, the original gray levels are indexes for the colormap, providing the image's pseudocolors. The colormap follows the $N \times 3$ format, where N is the number of colors, and the columns store R, G, and B values in the [0, 1.0] range.
3 Up to MATLAB 2019a colormaps' default number of colors was 64. From MATLAB 2019b it is 256.
4 Under ideal conditions, a human observer discriminates around one thousand shades of gray [16], against around two million colors [9].

Part IX

Batch processing and handling large images

Part IX – Batch processing and handling large images

The recipes in Part IX focus on two practical problems associated with the image processing pipeline that have become increasingly important in recent years: (1) handling very large images and (2) performing batch processing operations on a collection of images.

Recipe 29 shows how to handle gigapixel-sized images in MATLAB, using examples from digital pathology.

Recipe 30 shows how to streamline batch image processing operations both interactively as well as programmatically.

DOI: 10.1201/9781003170198-37

29

Recipe 29: Processing very large images

This recipe teaches you how to read, store, process, and display very large images using MATLAB.

Handling extremely large images presents significant challenges. These challenges can stem from the image's size exceeding memory capacity or from the image surpassing processing capabilities once loaded. Moreover, the storage and retrieval of such large images usually demand specialized hardware and software solutions to manage the data effectively.

This recipe demonstrates how to read, store, process, and display very large images. The focal point is the MATLAB `blockedImage` object that can be used to process images, volumes, or multidimensional images that are too large to fit into memory.

You will need (Ingredients)

- MATLAB R2021a or later
- MATLAB Image Processing Toolbox (IPT) version R2021a or later
- Image files: `tumor_091R.tif`[1]

Steps (Preparation)

The main steps for processing very large images are:

1. Load a blocked image into the workspace using `blockedImage`.
2. (OPTIONAL) Display the image using `bigimageshow`.
3. Creates a `blockedImageDatastore` object that manages a collection of image blocks of one or more `blockedImage` objects.
4. (OPTIONAL) Display the blocked image using `montage`.

DOI: 10.1201/9781003170198-38

5. Apply image processing operations on the blocked image, one block at a time, using the `apply` function.

6. Display the *before* and *after* images using `bigimageshow`.

The code in Listing 29.1 illustrates how to perform the first four steps of this recipe.

LISTING 29.1
Loading and displaying large images.

```
 1  % Loading and displaying large images
 2  file_name = 'tumor_091R.tif';
 3  % Store details about the original file
 4  file_info = imfinfo(file_name);
 5  % Create a blocked image
 6  tumor_image = blockedImage(file_name);
 7  % Display details of the blocked image at the command line.
 8  disp(tumor_image)
 9  % View the blocked image
10  bigimageshow(tumor_image)
11  % Inspect resolution levels
12  level_size_info = table((1:length(tumor_image.Size))', ...
13      tumor_image.Size(:,1), tumor_image.Size(:,2), ...
14      tumor_image.Size(:,1)./tumor_image.Size(:,2), ...
15      'VariableNames',["Resolution Level" "Image Width" ...
16      "Image Height" "Aspect Ratio"]);
17  disp(level_size_info)
18  % Create a blockedImageDatastore, specifying the resolution level
19  % and the blocksize.
20  bls = selectBlockLocations(tumor_image,'ExcludeIncompleteBlocks',true);
21  blocked_imds = blockedImageDatastore(tumor_image, "BlockLocationSet",
        bls);
22  %Read all the blocks in the datastore.
23  b = readall(blocked_imds);
24  % Display the big image with grid lines indicating blocks
25  figure, bigimageshow(tumor_image,...
26      'GridVisible','on', 'GridLevel', 1,...
27      'GridLineWidth', 2, 'GridColor','k','GridAlpha',0.3);
28  % Display the blocked image
29  figure, montage(b)
```

We start by inspecting the image file's properties (line 4). This is a multiresolution color image whose maximum resolution is $5000 \times 5358 \times 3$ pixels. Line 6 creates a variable `tumor_image` that reads the image file contents using the `blockedImage` function.

Line 8 produces the following message in the Command Window:

```
blockedImage with properties:

 Read only properties
             Source: "/../tumor_091R.tif"
            Adapter: [1×1 images.blocked.TIFF]
               Size: [3×3 double]
        SizeInBlocks: [3×3 double]
     ClassUnderlying: [3×1 string]

 Settable properties
          BlockSize: [3×3 double]
```

Let's explore the meaning of these properties of the `blockedImage` object [1]:

- `Adapter`: An object that reads and writes 2D blocked image data as a single TIFF file.
- `Size`: Image size at each level, specified as an $L \times N$ matrix of positive integers, where L is the number of resolution levels and N is the number of dimensions of the image. This image has three levels, ranging from $5000 \times 5358 \times 3$ to $625 \times 670 \times 3$ pixels.
- `SizeInBlocks`: Size, expressed as the number of blocks and specified as an $L \times N$ matrix of positive integers, where L is the number of resolution levels, and N is the number of dimensions. This image has three levels, ranging from $5 \times 6 \times 1$ to $1 \times 1 \times 1$ pixels.
- `ClassUnderlying`: Pixel data type, specified as a string array with L elements, where L is number of resolution levels. Each element in the array is the data type of a pixel from the corresponding resolution level. For this image, the data type across all levels is `uint8`.
- `BlockSize`: Block size, specified as an $L \times N$ matrix of positive integers, where L is the number of resolution levels and N is the number of dimensions. `BlockSize` serves as the default size of data loaded into main memory at any time. It is the smallest unit of data that can be manipulated with the `blockedImage` interface. For this image, the block size for levels 1 and 2 is $1024 \times 1024 \times 3$ pixels, whereas, for level 3, the block size is $625 \times 670 \times 3$ pixels.

Line 10 displays the image in a figure window, using the `bigimageshow` function.

Lines 12–17 display the image width and height at each level, producing the result below. Note that the aspect ratio can change slightly among levels.

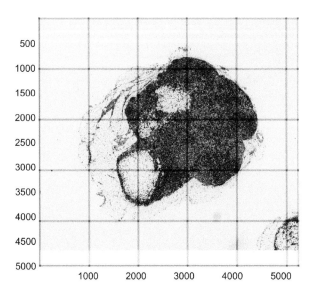

FIGURE 29.1
Viewing a large `blockedImage` with grid lines indicating blocks, using the `bigimageshow` function.

Resolution Level	Image Width	Image Height	Aspect Ratio
1	5000	5358	0.93318
2	1250	1340	0.93284
3	625	670	0.93284

Lines 20–21 create a `blockedImageDatastore` object, specifying the resolution level and the block size.

In line 23, we read all the data from the `blockedImageDatastore` and store it into a variable b, a cell array containing an element for every individual block.

Lines 25–27 display the image in a figure window, with grid lines indicating blocks (Figure 29.1).

Line 29 shows how to display the contents of the image from variable b, using the `montage` function (Figure 29.2). Note that since we chose to exclude incomplete blocks in line 20, the resulting image is a concatenation of the 20 *complete* blocks of size $1024 \times 1024 \times 3$ each. In other words, some of the contents at the bottom and the right portions of the original image have been lost.

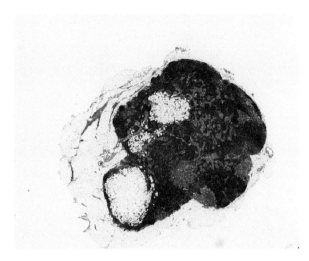

FIGURE 29.2
Viewing a large blockedImage using montage.

Using the code in Listing 29.2, we will show how to process the image blockwise using the apply function. This corresponds to steps 5 and 6 of this recipe.

LISTING 29.2
Processing large images in blockwise fashion.

```
%Processing large images in a blockwise fashion
%% Part 1 (Negative)
negative_img = apply(tumor_image, @(bs)imcomplement(bs.Data));
figure, bigimageshow(negative_img)

%% Part 2 (Edge detection)
edge_img = apply(tumor_image, @(bs)~edge(im2gray(bs.Data)));
figure, bigimageshow(edge_img) % undesirable blockiness effect

% Solving the blockiness problem
im_low_res = gather(tumor_image); % collect blocks from the coarsest level
[~, thresh] = edge(im2gray(im_low_res)); % learn threshold
edge_im_low_res = edge(im2gray(im_low_res),thresh); % test on coarse level
figure, imshow(edge_im_low_res)
% Validate on the largest image
edge_img_2 = apply(tumor_image,@(bs)~edge(im2gray(bs.Data),thresh));
% Visualize the result at the finest level
figure, bigimageshow(edge_img_2);
```

Line 3 shows how to compute the negative of a blockedImage in a block-by-block fashion[2] using the apply function. Everything works fine, as shown in Figure 29.3.

Next, we try to use the same code structure to extract the edges of the large image[3] in a blockwise fashion (see line 7). Alas, the result is not quite

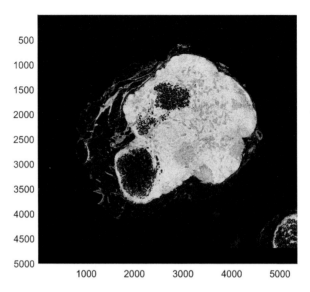

FIGURE 29.3
Negative of a `blockedImage` processed block-by-block.

what we expected, and there is a noticeable blockiness in the resulting image (Figure 29.4(a)). The reason behind the problem is that the default `edge` function uses a sensitivity threshold, which is computed for the entire image. Since, in our case, each block is processed as a separate image, different threshold values will be calculated for each block, hence the blockiness effect.

Lines 11–18 show an elegant way around this problem (inspired by [7]) that takes advantage of the multiple resolution levels in the image and the assumption that the distribution of individual pixel values should be roughly equal across all the levels. In line 11, we use the `gather` function to collect blocks from the coarsest level and use them to build an image, `im_low_res`, of size $625 \times 670 \times 3$ pixels. Line 12 shows how to run `edge` on the coarse image just to learn the automatically computed threshold and reuse that threshold in line 13. Upon inspecting the results for the coarse image (line 14), we validate the approach on the large image (line 16). Line 18 displays the results and allows us to confirm that the blockiness effect is gone, as expected (Figure 29.4(b)).

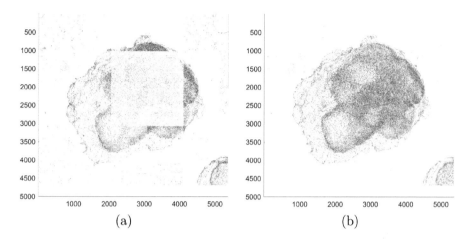

FIGURE 29.4
Edge detection results for a `blockedImage` processed block-by-block: (a) incorrect result (blockiness effect); (b) correct result.

Discussion (Recipe notes)

In this recipe, you learned several techniques for handling large images. The process can be very challenging, even using the `blockedImage` functionality from MATLAB.

By their very nature and size, gigapixel-sized images are inherently unwieldy. Moreover, additional complicating factors include the choice of block size and location, strategies for handling incomplete blocks, and performance considerations[4].

We strongly encourage exploring the resources in the *Learn more about it* section below for additional insights and examples.

Learn more about it

Useful MATLAB functions

Type the function name in the search field at www.mathworks.com/help/matlab/

· `compactitem` · `apply` · `bigimageshow` · `blockproc` · `blockedImage`
· `blockedImageDatastore` · `edge` · `gather` · `imcomplement` · `montage`
· `readall` · `selectBlockLocations` ·

MATLAB documentation, demos, and examples

- Block Processing Large Images
  www.mathworks.com/help/images/block-processing-large-images.
  html
- Block Size and Performance
  www.mathworks.com/help/images/block-size-and-performance.html
- Distinct Block Processing
  www.mathworks.com/help/images/distinct-block-processing.html
- Neighborhood or Block Processing: An Overview
  www.mathworks.com/help/images/neighborhood-or-block-processing-
  an-overview.html
- Parallel Block Processing on Large Image Files
  www.mathworks.com/help/images/parallel-block-processing-on-
  large-image-files.html
- Process Blocked Images Efficiently Using Partial Images or Lower
  Resolutions
  www.mathworks.com/help/images/process-big-image-efficiently.
  html
- Read Whole-Slide Images with Custom Blocked Image Adapter
  www.mathworks.com/help/images/read-whole-slide-images-with-
  custom-blocked-image-adapter.html

Notes

1   This image is a modified version of an image of a lymph node containing tumor
    tissue, tumor_091.tif, from the CAMELYON16 data set. The original image has
    eight resolution levels, and the finest level has a resolution of $53760 \times 61440 \times 3$
    pixels, i.e., 3.3 gigapixels. The modified image has only three coarse resolution
    levels and is substantially smaller, which allows for less demanding computational
    requirements.
2   When you run the code in MATLAB, some telltale signs that the processing is
    happening block by block include the appearance of a progress indicator (de-
    pending on image size and computational complexity of the operation) and the
    (column-wise) block-by-block rendering of the image using bigimageshow.
3   We chose to use the *negative* of the edge detection results, for better visualization
    on paper.
4   Processing large images in blockwise fashion can be done in parallel, if you have
    the appropriate hardware and the MATLAB *Parallel Computing Toolbox*.

30

Recipe 30: Batch processing a set of images

This recipe teaches you how to streamline an image processing workflow in MATLAB using batch processing techniques.

Batch image processing is a method of applying the same image processing operations to a large number of images at once. This process is often used in industries such as photography, graphic design, and web development, where large quantities of images need to be processed quickly and efficiently.

In MATLAB, batch image processing can be done interactively or programmatically. By processing images in batches, it becomes possible to automate and streamline tasks such as preprocessing, feature extraction, and analysis, saving time and computational resources in various applications.

You will need (Ingredients)

- MATLAB R2015a or later
- MATLAB Image Processing Toolbox (IPT) version R2015a or later
- Selected images from the PillQC data set [6]

Steps (Preparation)

Part 1: Processing a set of images programmatically

The main steps for applying the same image processing operation(s) on a set of images are:

1. Identify a folder containing the images that you want to process as a batch.
2. Create an array of file names containing the names of the image files in that folder.
3. Preallocate an array of appropriate size and read images into the array.
4. Process each image in the sequence using a function that implements the desired image processing operation.

DOI: 10.1201/9781003170198-39

5. (OPTIONAL) Display *before* and *after* images and visually evaluate the quality of the results.

Listing 30.1 illustrates the first three steps of this recipe, i.e., how to download and organize an image collection before any batch processing.

We use the PillQC data set, available on GitHub [6]. This data set is typically used to train and test image anomaly detection deep learning models [3]. It contains images from three classes: 149 *normal* images without defects, 43 *chip* images with chip defects in the pills, and 138 *dirt* images with dirt contamination. For this example, we will only use the 43 images from the *chip* subfolder.

Lines 3–19 contain code for downloading the dataset and organizing the images into subfolders under the folder whose path is stored in the image_dir variable. Lines 22–26 create a cell array of filenames. Lines 29–36 create a 4D variable input_batch to store the images. In this particular case, since there are 43 RGB images of 225×225 pixels each, the size of the input_batch variable is $225 \times 225 \times 3 \times 43$.

LISTING 30.1
Downloading and organizing an image collection for batch processing.

```
 1  % Downloading and organizing an image collection for batch processing
 2  %% Download PillQC dataset
 3  data_dir = fullfile('./',"PillQCdataset");
 4
 5  if ~exist(data_dir,"dir")
 6      mkdir(data_dir);
 7  end
 8
 9  image_dir = fullfile(data_dir,"/pillQC-main");
10
11  if ~exist(image_dir,"dir")
12      disp("Downloading Pill QC data set.");
13      disp("This can take several minutes to download and unzip...");
14      unzip("https://github.com/matlab-deep-learning/pillQC/archive/" + ...
15      "refs/heads/main.zip", data_dir);
16      delete(fullfile(image_dir,"*.m"),fullfile(image_dir,"*.mlx"), ...
17      fullfile(image_dir,"*.mat"),fullfile(image_dir,"*.md"));
18      disp("Done.");
19  end
20
21  %% Create array of filenames
22  file_folder = fullfile(image_dir,'images','chip');
23  dir_output = dir(fullfile(file_folder,'*.jpg'));
24
25  file_names = {dir_output.name}'
26  num_images = numel(file_names)
27
28  %% Preallocate an (m x n x 3 x p) array and read images into the array
29  cd(file_folder)
30  img = imread(file_names{1});
31  input_batch = zeros([size(img) num_images],class(img));
32  input_batch(:,:,:,1) = img;
33
34  for p = 2:num_images
35      input_batch(:,:,:,p) = imread(file_names{p});
36  end
```

The code in Listing 30.2 illustrates how to perform two separate operations – histogram equalization and binarization – on a sequence of images.

LISTING 30.2
Examples of batch processing: histogram equalization and binarization.

```
1  % Examples of batch processing
2  %% Part 1: histogram equalization
3  output_batch = histeq(input_batch);
4
5  % View each image pair (before/after processing)
6  figure;
7  for k = 1:num_images
8      imshow(input_batch(:,:,:,k));
9      title(sprintf('Original Image # %d',k));
10     pause(1);
11     imshow(output_batch(:,:,:,k));
12     title(sprintf('Processed Image # %d',k));
13     pause(1);
14 end
15
16 %% Part 2: binarization
17 for p = 1:num_images
18     output_batch_2(:,:,p) = imbinarize(im2gray(input_batch(:,:,:,p)));
19 end
20
21 % View original and processed images
22 figure, montage(input_batch)
23 figure, montage(output_batch_2)
```

In line 3, we perform histogram equalization across the entire batch in a single line of code. This is possible because both input and output images are RGB images, i.e., they have the same number of dimensions. Lines 6–14 show how we can visualize the results for all images in the batch in a loop that alternates between the input and output image every second or so.

When the image processing operation results in an image of different dimensions (e.g., the input is an RGB image, and the output is a grayscale image), we have to process each image inside a loop (lines 17–19) so that each RGB image is processed separately and the result is assigned to a variable output_batch_2 whose dimensions are $m \times n \times p$, where $m = n = 225$ and $p = 43$ in this case.

Lines 22–23 show how to exhibit all images before and after batch binarization (Figure 30.1).

Part 2: Batch processing a set of images interactively

The *Image Batch Processor* App provides a convenient way to process a batch of images in a semi-automated way. Similarly to other MATLAB apps, it

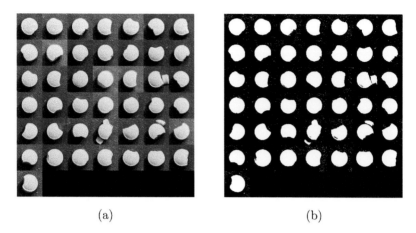

(a)   (b)

FIGURE 30.1
Batch processing of 43 images: (a) original images; (b) binarized images.

offers a rich GUI for initial setup and interactive experimentation and visualization of results that also allows you to export the processed images and the processing pipeline for future reuse in a purely programmatic way.

The main steps for using the *Image Batch Processor* App[1] are:

1. Identify a folder containing the images that you want to process as a batch.
2. Open the *Image Batch Processor* App.
3. Load images from the folder of interest into the *Image Batch Processor* App.
4. Specify batch processing function.
5. Process images using batch processing function.
6. Visualize results.
7. Export processed images and processing pipeline.

We will use the same data set and folder structure as Part 1. After opening the *Image Batch Processor* App from the MATLAB toolstrip (under the *Image Processing and Computer Vision* section), you should see a GUI that looks like the one in Figure 30.2.

FIGURE 30.2
Image Batch Processor App: initial GUI.

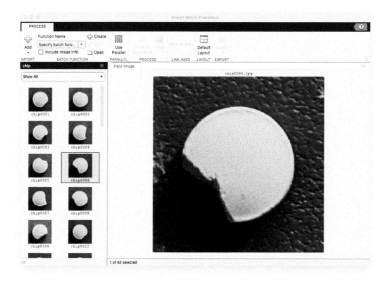

FIGURE 30.3
Snapshot of the *Image Batch Processor* App after selecting the *chip* folder and a particular image for detailed inspection.

Click on the *Add* button, locate and select the *chip* folder containing the same 43 images used earlier in this recipe. You should see a screen similar to the one shown in Figure 30.3.

Next, click on the *Create* button to create a new batch processing function using a template. This will take you to the MATLAB editor, where you'll see a template function my imfcn that looks like Listing 30.3[2].

LISTING 30.3
Batch processing: image binarization using an autogenerated template function.

```
function results = myimfcn(varargin)
% Image Processing Function
% VARARGIN - Can contain up to two inputs:
%   IM - First input is a numeric array containing the image data.
%   INFO - Second input is a scalar structure containing information about
%          the input image source.
```

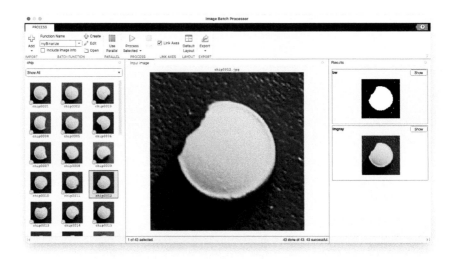

FIGURE 30.4
Snapshot of the *Image Batch Processor* App after processing the batch using the default function.

```
 7  %    RESULTS - A scalar struct with the processing results.
 8
 9  %-----------------------
10  % Auto-generated by imageBatchProcessor App.
11  % When used by the App, this function will be called
12  % for each input image file automatically.
13  %-----------------------
14
15  % Input parsing
16  im = varargin{1};
17  if nargin == 2
18      % Obtain information about the input image source
19      info = varargin{2};
20  end
21  %-----------------------
22  % Replace the sample below with your code
23  imgray = im2gray(im);
24  bw = imbinarize(imgray);
25  results.imgray = imgray;
26  results.bw      = bw;
27  %-----------------------
```

We will use the template function to have a feel for the way the app performs the batch processing and displays the results. Select the *Process All* button on the drop-down menu of the "green play" button and click on it. You will get the results at the GUI, as shown in Figure 30.4. Note that the default function creates two variables, imgray and bw, which can be displayed, saved, and used separately if needed.

Next, we will edit this function to add a post-processing step to remove spurious pixels from the binarized image. We chose to apply a morphological opening operation using a disk-shaped structuring element[3]. The resulting image, bwClean, is now part of the results of the batch operation. The modified function is shown in Listing 30.4.

LISTING 30.4

Batch processing: modified image binarization function.

```
function results = myBinarize(varargin)

% Input parsing
im = varargin{1};

if nargin == 2
    % Obtain information about the input image source
    info = varargin{2};
end

% Our code
imgray = im2gray(im); % Convert to grayscale
bw = imbinarize(imgray); % Binarize
bwClean = imopen(bw,strel("disk",3,4)); % Remove spurious pixels

results.imgray = imgray;
results.bw      = bw;
results.bwClean = bwClean;
```

After running the modified function across all 43 images, we can browse the results. Figure 30.5 shows the details for a particular image whose original file name is chip0005.jpg. The same figure shows the three options available under the *Export* button. For the next step, we will export the result of all processed images to the workspace using the options indicated in Figure 30.6.

Next, we will use the code in Listing 30.5 to convert the table to an array (line 1), create separate variables for all images (original, gray, bw, and bwClean) (lines 2–7), and display all images in a montage (Figure 30.7).

LISTING 30.5

Postprocessing and displaying results of batch processing.

```
A = table2array(allresults);
imgNumber = 5;
bw = A{imgNumber,1};
bwClean = A{imgNumber,2};
gray = A{imgNumber,3};
originalFileName = A{imgNumber,4};
original = imread(originalFileName);

montage({original, gray, bw, bwClean})
```

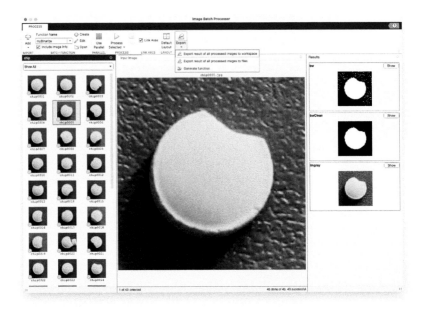

FIGURE 30.5
Snapshot of the *Image Batch Processor* App after processing the batch using the modified function and getting ready to export the results.

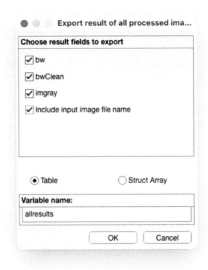

FIGURE 30.6
Export options: choosing all fields and selecting a `table` as the data structure for variable `all-results`.

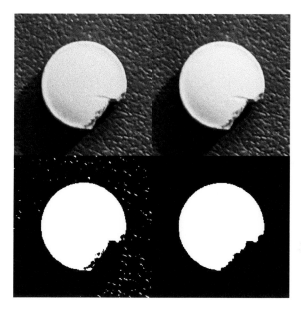

FIGURE 30.7
Montage for an example image: original, grayscale, binarized, and post-processed.

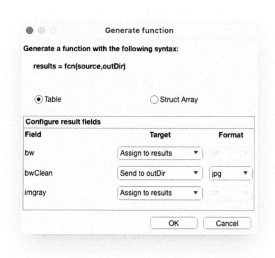

FIGURE 30.8
Generate function options. Note that in this case, we chose to save the final result (bwClean) as JPG files in the directory specified as outDir.

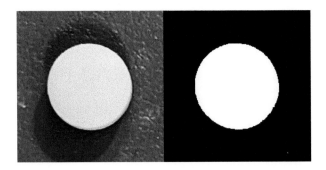

FIGURE 30.9
Example of batch processing for a *normal* chip image.

Lastly, we will click on the *Export* button one more time and select the *Generate function* option. This opens a dialog box (Figure 30.8) and creates a customized function to be used next time we need to perform the same operations on another set of images. The resulting function is called `batchmyBinarize` and has more than 500 (!) lines of code.

The code in Listing 30.6 shows how the generated function can be used to apply the same image processing pipeline to the images in another image collection, in this case, the *normal* subfolder of the data set. Lines 1–2 configure the source and output folders, line 4 calls the batch processing function, and lines 5–7 display the result for a particular image (Figure 30.9).

LISTING 30.6
Reusing a function for batch processing on another image collection.

```
sourceDir = "./PillQCdataset/pillQC-main/images/normal";
outputDir = fullfile(sourceDir,'results');

result = batchmyBinarize(sourceDir, outputDir);
exampleInput = imread(fullfile(sourceDir,'normal0024.jpg'));
exampleOutput = imread(fullfile(sourceDir,'normal0024_bwClean.tiff'));
montage({exampleInput exampleOutput})
```

Discussion (Recipe notes)

The ability to process images in batch mode is a time saver for numerous image processing applications where images come from the same source (sensor, camera, microscope) and have similar characteristics (size, number of colors, file format, etc.).

In this recipe, you learned several ways to perform batch processing operations with different levels of interactivity involved in the process. In practice, you might want to use the interactive mode to test how well a certain image processing operation (or pipeline) works on a set of images and then export the code for applying the same methods to other sets of images programmatically.

Learn more about it

Useful MATLAB functions

Type the function name in the search field at `www.mathworks.com/help/matlab/`

· `imageBatchProcessor` · `table2array` ·

MATLAB documentation, demos, and examples

- Image Batch Processor App
  `www.mathworks.com/help/images/ref/imagebatchprocessor-app.html`
- Perform an Operation on a Sequence of Images
  `www.mathworks.com/help/images/process-image-sequences.html`
- Process Folder of Images Using Image Batch Processor App
  `www.mathworks.com/help/images/batch-processing-using-the-image-batch-processor-app.html`
- View Image Sequences in Video Viewer
  `www.mathworks.com/help/images/view-image-sequences-in-video-viewer-app.html`
- Work with Image Sequences as Multidimensional Arrays
  `www.mathworks.com/help/images/what-is-an-image-sequence.html`

Notes

1 Since R2023a, MATLAB supports opening the *Image Batch Processor* and loading images stored in a specific folder (or image datastore) in a single line in the command window. Therefore, steps 1–3 have become a single line of code.
2 Some lines were omitted for space reasons.
3 See Recipe 24.

Bibliography

1. Big or multiresolution image made from discrete blocks - MATLAB. `www.math works.com/help/images/ref/blockedimage.html`. (Accessed on 2023-07-07).

2. CIE | International Commission on Illumination / Comission Internationale de L'eclairage / Internationale Beleuchtungskommission `http://cie.co.at/`. (Accessed on 2023-08-28).

3. Detect image anomalies using explainable fcdd network - MATLAB & Simulink. `www.mathworks.com/help/vision/ug/detect-image-anomalies-using-explainable-one-class-classification-neural-network.html`. (Accessed on 2023-07-08).

4. How to posterize a photo in photoshop - Adobe. `www.adobe.com/creativecloud/photography/discover/posterize-photo.html`. (Accessed on 2023-07-06).

5. HSL and HSV - Wikipedia. `https://en.wikipedia.org/wiki/HSL_and_HSV`. (Accessed on 2023-08-28).

6. A pill quality control dataset and associated anomaly detection example. `https://github.com/matlab-deep-learning/pillQC`. (Accessed on 2023-07-08).

7. Process blocked images efficiently using partial images or lower resolutions - MATLAB & Simulink. `www.mathworks.com/help/images/process-big-image-efficiently.html`. (Accessed on 2023-07-08).

8. Parameter values for ultra-high definition television systems for production and international programme exchange. ITU-R Recommendation BT.2020-1, 2015.

9. J. M. M. Linhares, P. D. Pinto, and S. M. C. Nascimento. The number of discernible colors in natural scenes. *J. Opt. Soc. Am. A*, 25(12):2918–2924, Dec 2008.

10. W. Burger and M. J. Burge. *Digital Image Processing: an algorithmic introduction using Java*. Springer, New York, 2008.

11. X. Dong, G. Wang, Y. Pang, W. Li, J. Wen, W. Meng, and Y. Lu. Fast efficient algorithm for enhancement of low lighting video. In *2011 IEEE International Conference on Multimedia and Expo*, pages 1–6, 2011.

12. R. C. Gonzalez and R. E. Woods. *Digital Image Processing*. Prentice-Hall, Upper Saddle River, NJ, third edition, 2008.

13. A. K. Jain. *Fundamentals of Digital Image Processing*. Prentice-Hall, Englewood Cliffs, 1989.

14. M. Kamlet. Nasa captures first air-to-air images of supersonic shockwave interaction in flight. www.nasa.gov/centers/armstrong/features/supersonic-shockwave-interaction.html. (Accessed on 2023-25-08).

15. M. Kass, A. Witkin, and D. Terzopoulos. Snakes: Active contour models. *International journal of computer vision*, 1(4):321–331, 1988.

16. T. Kimpe and T. Tuytschaever. Increasing the number of gray shades in medical display systems—how much is enough? *Journal of digital imaging*, 20(4):422–432, 2007.

17. Li Fei-Fei, R. Fergus, and P. Perona. Learning generative visual models from few training examples: an incremental bayesian approach tested on 101 object categories. In *2004 Conference on Computer Vision and Pattern Recognition Workshop*, pages 178–178, 2004.

18. O. Marques. *Practical Image and Video Processing Using MATLAB*. Wiley - IEEE. Wiley, 2011.

19. N. Otsu.   A threshold selection method from gray-level histograms.   *IEEE Transactions on Systems, Man, and Cybernetics*, 9(1):62–66, 1979.

20. C. Poynton. *Digital Video and HDTV Algorithms and Interfaces*. Morgan Kaufmann Publishers, San Francisco, 2003.

21. W. K. Pratt. *Digital Image Processing*. New York: Wiley, fourth edition, 2007.

22. E. Reinhard, E. A. Khan, A. O. Akyz, and G. M. Johnson.   *Color Imaging: Fundamentals and Applications*. A. K. Peters, Ltd., USA, 2008.

23. R. Szeliski. *Computer Vision Algorithms and Applications*. Springer, London; New York, 2011.

24. A. Zeileis, J. C. Fisher, K. Hornik, R. Ihaka, C. D. McWhite, P. Murrell, R. Stauffer, and C. O. Wilke. colorspace: A toolbox for manipulating and assessing colors and palettes. *Journal of Statistical Software*, 96(1):1–49, 2020.

25. A. Zeileis, K. Hornik, and P. Murrell. Escaping RGBland: Selecting colors for statistical graphics.   *Computational Statistics & Data Analysis*, 53(9):3259–3270, 2009.

26. K. Zuiderveld. Contrast limited adaptive histogram equalization. *Graphics gems*, pages 474–485, 1994.

Index